# MANAGEMENT:

## *READY*

## *AIM*

## *FIRE*

by

Anthony C. La Russo

author**HOUSE**™

1663 LIBERTY DRIVE, SUITE 200
BLOOMINGTON, INDIANA 47403
(800) 839-8640
WWW.AUTHORHOUSE.COM

First published by AuthorHouse 09/20/05


ISBN: 1-4208-3790-7 (sc)


Library of Congress Control Number: 2005902385

Printed in the United States of America
Bloomington, Indiana

This book is printed on acid-free paper.

# TABLE OF CONTENTS

## CHAPTER 6   PARTICIPATIVE MANAGEMENT - NO FREE LUNCH

## CHAPTER 7   CONCLUDING THOUGHTS - WORK BOOK

# FIGURES & TABLES

# INTRODUCTION

It is easy to think that, due to the rapid changes in technology, the globalization of markets and the complex and dangerous world political picture, we need to find new management theories without which we are lost! In reality we need to find ways to implement and build upon existing sound theories and concepts. Recent failures such as Enron, et al, the bursting of the Tech Bubble and even the space shuttle accident and the subsequent report on NASA, continue to make this clear. Which of these would have occurred if sound management practices had been implemented?

The basic management functions of organizing, leading, planning and controlling may need to be somewhat redefined and more difficult to practice given the speed of the environment, but historic models continue to provide a foundation for the future. The references noted in this book are intended to serve two purposes. First, to demonstrate that it is often not a lack of knowledge that constrains us, but a lack of action (just look at the dates of the works). Second, to assist the interested reader in gaining further insights. By no means are these works the only ones in their field, but it's a start.

The one factor in the management equation that has permanently changed is the speed of everything in our lives. This necessitates that we better understand and improve upon our ability to practice the basic functions of management. To do this a system must exist to identify and anticipate opportunities and threats, and to focus the organization's resources. It has often been said in sports that "speed kills." In business speed has become your best weapon and greatest concern. Here, too, speed kills.

It may be helpful to view the practice of management in 3 phases:

| READY | Think, Plan, Lead and Communicate |
|---|---|
| AIM | Focus and Organize |
| FIRE | Commit, Implement and Keep Everyone Involved |

Twenty years ago I began an article reminding readers that the ancient Chinese believed the most severe curse was to be condemned to live in interesting times. These times were defined as being fraught with rapid change and turmoil.

Well, it appears we have been cursed. So how do we prosper in this environment?

Note: Terms such as he or she/his or hers are not meant to be specific to either gender. To demonstrate this, such terms have been used interchangeably throughout the book.

# CHAPTER 1
## NAVIGATING UNCHARTED WATERS

Summary

One of the most obvious difficulties a manager faces today is the unparalleled expansion of his environment. Prior training and experience have often not prepared managers for the world they now face. Lack of behavioral models, or, even worse, incorrect models, do not provide the security that was available to prior generations.

The lack of preparation has turned a turbulent environment into a hostile one for managers. Today's managers often find themselves in a "catch-up" process regarding changes in technology, market trends, competitors, etc. This can be very costly, not only for the individual but for the entire organization.

Senior management must commit to invest in the members of their organization. Such an investment can take the shape of formal training, a planned job rotation process, etc. However, it can only be accomplished in an environment which rewards successes and allows for failures based on reasonable initiatives. In the short-term, these actions may reduce efficiency, but, if an organization is to survive and grow, it must make an active commitment to increase its members' skills and to tap their creativity.

Due to profit pressures caused by global competition and rising costs, it has become increasingly difficult for organizations to commit to longer range investments in people. This comes precisely at a time when they are most needed. As discussed later, programs can be established under different management philosophies.

**It is essential that management be honest with its members as to the goals and consequences of any long-term program.**

Managers continue to look for models and rules to help guide their behavior. Confusion has led to a pattern of reacting to crises as they occur rather than anticipating events. As a result, managers can find that they have set a long-term path for their organization by making a series of decisions focusing on numerous separate short-term problems.

**Decisions made without an understanding of their relationship to each other and their longer term effects can result in an unintended and unrecognized strategy.**

Remember, all organizations have a strategy, whether it is intentional or results from a series of day-to-day decisions. An unintended strategy can be fatal, since it may be invisible for a considerable period of time and can even be in direct conflict with management's stated goals.

<u>Expanding Environment</u>

A series of socio-economic trends has resulted in significant changes to the environment. While it is easy, and at times popular, to exaggerate their impact, it is clear that they have permanently enlarged management's role. In addition, subtle changes such as an increasing emphasis on protecting employees'/people's rights despite decreased union strength will continue to quietly influence the environment.

Managers must be more concerned and alert to changes in their surroundings. This requires efficient use of ever increasing amounts of information. Unlike prior periods, managers today frequently have sufficient data, but, despite technological advancements, often do not have an efficient system for collecting, analyzing and distributing information.

The development of mini computers and rapid communication systems can lead managers to become involved in excessive activities to gather and analyze data rather than manage information.

Today's volatile environment has placed new importance and stress on an organization's information systems. The availability of quality information on a timely basis is and will continue to be a significant asset. All organizations claim to believe such statements, but successful ones commit to the reality. Information can provide an organization with a competitive advantage both as it attempts to behave opportunistically in the short-run and implement long-term programs.

---

**An organization cannot afford to become paralyzed either by an insufficient amount or an unmanaged glut of data.**

---

Global Competition

Products from America's basic industries face reduced rates of growth in aggregate demand and increased competition. In addition, these industries have often been managed based on lower unit production costs through economies of scale which have been misinterpreted as productivity gains. While economies of scale result in lower costs at higher production levels, a true productivity gain occurs when the cost of producing at a given level is less than it previously was at that level. Therefore, as demand for products from these industries declines, costs increase, leading to a further deterioration of an organization's competitiveness.

High tech organizations can find themselves with limited resources, including experience, large R&D expenditures and markets in which products can become obsolete apparently overnight. Advances in technology and lifestyle changes have shortened product life cycles at record speed. This has increased the need to provide an organization with a flow of ideas which have an acceptable chance of developing into products, and the ability to quickly commercialize them. Due to the increased attention being paid to specialized or niche products, competition is fierce on all fronts, both from traditional sources and new entries.

All organizations are faced with growing competition as a result of the maturing of traditional markets, as well as the emergence of an increasingly global economy. Businesses have been forced to look beyond their usual markets for sales outlets and are faced with new competitors. Often these competitors have more experience in functioning in a worldwide marketplace, as well as a natural

3

and/or artificial (direct government assistance, tariff barriers, etc.) comparative advantage.

Never before has it been as important for management to question the reasons for its organization's existence. At the upper levels, managers must ask themselves questions such as: "Why should my organization exist? What can we provide that others do not or cannot provide in the marketplace?" Management needs to revisit the advice provided decades ago by Peter F. Drucker when he noted that the mission and purpose of every business is to satisfy the customer.[1] At lower levels in the organization, managers need to question the reason for their departments and staffing. This open process is essential to be able to develop an organization for the future.

## Updating Views and Skills

The primary task of a manager is to fully utilize the factors of production. To do this, managers must anticipate and, when possible, influence events to position their organizations to benefit from them.

---

**Frequently, prior experience and formal training have taught managers "to do" and not to think or plan for the future.**

---

We have all been told about the "shirt-sleeve" managers who "dig in" and work alongside their staff. While this may be appropriate from time to time, if this description becomes a role model, it can be dangerous. Such a focus can lead managers into a "business as usual" pattern of behavior. Cluttering a manager's overall view with only the day-to-day will narrow her focus and result in a disproportionate emphasis on short-term results. Managers can become so intent on receiving instant feedback from their actions they miss a key part of their role. Those who do the same work as non-managers can be a hidden liability to their organization. However, organizations have frequently rewarded this type of behavior. In some instances I have seen them become almost part of a folk lore.

A misunderstanding of management's role comes about from a strong emphasis on short-term results. This may be direct, as a result of a specific decision(s), or, probably more often, indirect.

**Managers typically have little free time to focus on performing their basic managerial functions of planning, organizing, leading and controlling. Their days are usually filled with meeting near-term deadlines and a series of unplanned but continuous interruptions.**

During an average week, it is not uncommon for managers to spend more than half of their time in meetings, the vast majority of which are called by others; and/or on the phone, with a significant portion of the remaining time used to produce reports. Hand-held technology has even taken away travel periods, which previously could be used to escape the day-to-day. Some organizations find it unacceptable for a person not to be in almost constant communication with others; just look at the explosion in e-mails. This behavior forces or teaches managers to react to crises while under pressure rather than anticipate problems.

In addition to pressures resulting from a desire for instant gratification, emphasis on short-term results can come from the investment community and an organization's compensation system. Management can become overly concerned with the immediate reaction of the financial markets to short-term results, while not paying adequate attention to the longer-term effects of decisions. Due to the influence of shareholders and outsiders and the relative ease of measuring near-term results, a significant portion of a person's compensation is often based on the short-term and/or stock (equity) price. This may teach managers that their job is to assure short-term success even at the possible expense of long-term growth.

Such a limited focus helps to explain the actions of the foreman who forgoes routine maintenance to hold down costs while shortening the life of a major asset; the middle manager who "cooks the books" without the knowledge of his supervisor, to report results he perceives his supervisor will find acceptable, or possibly influencing senior managements' decision to spend mega dollars to financially engineer their company's stock price, via stock buybacks, while reducing R&D expenditures. None of the above are meant to address the extreme situations demonstrated by companies such as Enron, WorldCom, Global Crossing, etc. But, there certainly appears to be a strong correlation between rewards and management's activities even in these cases.

Managers who are overly concerned with short-term results or "doing today's task" cannot anticipate and influence future events and position their organization to benefit from them. To fulfill the proper role of management requires an active pursuit of the fundamental functions of planning, leading, organizing and controlling. Such a commitment, however, will only be present when it is visibly encouraged by the organization.

---

**The more volatile the environment, the greater the need to recognize the distinct role of management. Although rarely openly talked about, one of the hardest things in an organization is maintaining long-term goals, discipline and energy.**

---

While the four basic management functions have not changed, the skills required to practice them successfully have. Even managers with extensive formal training may not be properly prepared for the environment they currently face. While traditional graduate business training tends to stress analytical ability, it often does not sufficiently improve interpersonal and administrative skills. Also, as a result of having "played" senior executive in graduate school, the expectations of new recruits may be far too high for their initial entry into an organization. This can cause frustration on their part, which will hinder their ability to develop needed skills.

Search for Role Models

The increasing discomfort caused by a lack of appropriate training in traditional organizations has resulted in considerable attention being devoted to identifying "excellent companies" and isolating characteristics which they have in common.[2] Despite this effort, the task of identifying currently prosperous companies which continue to prosper in the future has proven more difficult than might be expected. However, such work has brought about a widespread awareness that successful organizations, in different businesses, do share some basic characteristics. These findings have begun to provide the needed role models.

Care is required when looking at common characteristics of selected organizations. Often, these lists look like little more than "a return to basics." Furthermore, a large number of unsuccessful organizations would probably state that they agree with these steps/ views and also have tried to implement them. It is not the knowledge of these characteristics which make a company successful, but its management's ability to organize the efforts of its participants in carrying out the required tasks.

---

**Creation of an environment which encourages people to perform tasks not to any given specification but to continuing levels of improvement results in a prosperous organization.**

---

Common Characteristics

Despite the best efforts of numerous people, no list of common characteristics can be all inclusive. By reviewing prior works, as well as conducting a less formal review of many organizations, the basis for establishing a list of the more obvious characteristics is available. These include:

• People are seen as the prime source of productivity increases.

• Participants share an identified sense of purpose concerning their activities and those of the organization.

• Encouragement of members to experiment to improve current procedures or products, and within limits, tolerance of failure.

• Existence of systems to reward individuals and groups.

• Strong emphasis on quality.

• Knowledge of the organization's markets including customers, competitors, products and substitute products.

• Information is viewed as an asset to be contributed to, shared and used.

• A decision making, action oriented management and an understanding of the process, with a willingness to make difficult/ unpleasant decisions.

Management of a successful organization must ask itself several questions, and, once answered, act upon these responses. These "what" questions include:

• What do I bring to the market which is or would be missing?

• What are my major assets?

• What are my key means to compete?

• What structure is necessary to assure timely information and decisions?

Honest answers to these and similar questions will focus management's attention on developing characteristics which will sustain their organization.

---

**It should always be remembered that "better organizations" look at themselves as having a virtually infinite life, and establish systems which will perpetuate the life of the organization beyond that of any individual or group.**

---

These systems need to be flexible to allow for modifications over an extended period and strong enough to compensate for the occasional poor manager.

Such a long-term view encourages managers to seek opportunities for building businesses rather than being preoccupied with short-term results. This view stresses the value of developing a business with strategic advantages versus the competition, rather than solely pursuing "quick fix" answers such as acquisitions. The latter approach can result from a desire by management for instant returns. However, in a large number of cases, this approach has failed due to a lack of knowledge about the newly acquired business, overextension of the acquiring organization's resources, paying too high an initial price and a general lack of attention to people issues. Better managed organizations look at an acquisition as only one possible means of entering a new business or enhancing an existing position.

Shared Purpose

An initial requirement for forming an effective team is an "understanding, mutual agreement, and identification with respect to the primary task."[3] A first step in this process is the existence of a clear statement of what business(es) an organization intends to be in and how it will conduct itself. A basic statement to provide guidance, particularly during times of severe change, can be vital in identifying and sharing a common set of goals, as well as keeping management focused.

In order for all participants to work toward a goal, it must not only be clearly identified but also be seen as being consistent with the individual's goals. Therefore, the organization's members need to recognize that their long-term interests are best served by having the organization obtain its goals. While there will be periods of time during which the two sets of goals appear in conflict, these occurrences must be relatively infrequent and short-lived. That is one of the reasons a quick, well planned downsizing is more efficient than a prolonged series of unannounced actions. It limits the period of conflict and uncertainty.

Managers need to understand that the organization's goals and those of its members must be viewed by participants as being compatible. While I have never heard anyone directly argue against this premise as an "ideal", a spectator might question how widely the belief is truly held. The situation is further complicated by circumstances organizations face today such as:

• Excess global production capacity for an increasing list of products, resulting in cutbacks and facility closures in higher cost countries, such as the U.S.

• Productivity gains that translate into needed profits but fewer jobs.

• Decisions to harvest business units in higher cost countries and invest the funds generated in other countries.

• Reduction in dividend taxes which provides members of senior management who are more likely to own equity with, at times, a sizeable pay increase, while others in the organization lose jobs, or receive pay increases below historic levels. I am not arguing for or against the recent tax changes, only noting a fact.

As a member of management of several organizations for over three decades, I am aware of the realities management faces. Even steps which may produce future gains can cause near-term conflict. Managing these conflicting realities is discussed throughout, particularly in Chapter 6.

People must believe that they are being treated fairly; that is, that one group is not being asked to sacrifice to a greater degree than other groups. Destructive rivalries between groups will emerge once it is perceived that one group is not being treated fairly compared to others, or that a group can only "win" at the expense of another. This need not be a classic "management vs. employee" conflict but can be, and often is, between peer groups within the ranks of "employees" or "management." Note that the word "fairly" has been used and not the word "equally."

**It is a mistake for managers to believe that equal treatment is fair. In fact, by treating everyone equally, you punish the better performers and reward poor ones.**

People, Productivity and Reward Systems

Successful organizations view people as their key assets and the primary source of productivity increases. These organizations provide an environment which encourages experimentation to improve procedures and products, rewards success and, within limits, tolerates failure. This can be done in a variety of ways. It is important that a system exists and has the outward support of senior management. Successful organizations realize that statements by company officials regarding the importance of everyone's contribution without the known existence of support systems can result in lowering morale.

Better companies recognize that productivity increases result from two sources: (1) increased worker education/skills and (2) improved work procedures, coupled with technological innovation. Without skilled people and sound procedures, technological innovation may not improve productivity. In fact, it can decrease productivity due to the lack of acceptance or improper use.

**Better managed organizations are not seduced by improved technology but view it as a means, when applied as part of a well planned environment, to increase productivity. Ultimately, people's imagination and dedication to solving problems are the real source of all productivity gains.**

While compensation is one of the largest expenses in most organizations, it was not until fairly recently that many organizations began to systematically evaluate compensation policies as a strategic factor in attaining goals. Like all other activities, it is not the aggregate amount of expenditures which is important but the manner in which the funds are spent. For some reason, however, this point can escape management's attention.

Reward systems are the primary mechanism whereby management shows the members what is expected of them, provides positive reinforcement for acceptable acts and negative responses to unacceptable actions. Successful management takes the time and considerable effort to identify those activities which are key to the organization's success and at least attempts to measure an individual's and group's results at these activities.

---

**Regardless of what is said by management, people will respond to signals provided by their organization's compensation system.**

---

For an organization to provide the correct signals, it must have a clear view of its goals and the necessary steps to achieve them. This overall view is then broken down to discrete activities for all levels within the organization. The process is often complicated by the fact that most large organizations have more than a single business unit. Each will have a series of goals, which can be quite different and require different compensation schemes.

Compensation systems and their effects on the people are a dynamic process which can greatly assist in attaining or frustrating an organization's goals. Frequently the impact of a compensation scheme is subtle and therefore the effects of an improper plan may escape detection by management for some time. Better managed companies recognize the potential impact of compensation and strive to implement systems which are consistent with the organization's goals.

People will ultimately respond to a system of rewards and punishments regardless of the organization's intended goals. For example, if the development of new products or procedures is thought to be an important activity but people are compensated based on production, day-to-day production activities are likely to receive the lion's share of attention. Furthermore, if individuals are punished for unsuccessful ideas, regardless of their apparent merit when initiated, and rewarded for successful efforts, even if they have relatively little impact, they are likely to respond by applying their efforts to safer areas where success is more likely, and to stay away from higher risk, but potentially higher return activities.

The traditional accounting system provides the data for many organizational decisions, including executive compensation. This system produces reports containing variances from budgets, forecasts and prior periods. Where does the typical organization measure the cost of lost opportunities due to an inappropriate action or no action? Many of our standard systems/practices can place an emphasis on consistency even at the expense of growth. Reward systems based on short-term results, such as quarterly profits, may increase profits today, but perhaps at a future expense.

---

**Compensation systems are likely to get the results they are aimed at. So be careful to select targets well.**

---

Value of Information and Market Knowledge

Successful organizations understand the value of information and the competitive advantage it can provide. These organizations have known systems to collect and analyze data and distribute information to the various levels of decision makers. In order for data to become valuable, it must be provided to internal customers on a timely basis and in a manner which assists in the decision making process.

Although executives agree about the importance of competitor information, the necessary commitment by the organization to gather and process data may not be present. A survey taken in 1973 of executives concerning the need and use of competitor information pointed out an interesting relationship between the importance managers said they placed on such information and their dedication to gathering and using it. Although this survey is old, because of the thoroughness of the work, including a comparison to earlier results, its findings are worth considering.[4]

When asked "Do you think your company should have a more systematic method of gathering, processing, analyzing, and reporting information about competitors?" 72% answered yes (definitely 37%; probably 35%.) This compared to a 57% affirmative response in 1959. However, when asked about the type of systems used to gather competitor information, only 8% had formal departments and a second 8% performed regular reporting without a formal department. The most common response (1973 - 43%; 1959 - 28%) was that reporting was done on an "as needed basis." Therefore, while the majority of managers questioned in 1959 and 1973 had an awareness of the importance of competitive information, despite the passage of time, relatively little organizational change appears to have taken place.

The results of a more recent, but still dated, survey published in 1988 by The Conference Board, Inc. continues to provide evidence that recognition of the importance of competitive information does not automatically result in action by management to treat it as an asset.[5] While 98% of the survey respondents viewed monitoring competitors' activities as important (very 68%; fairly 30%), only 37% thought that their organization had a well-developed monitoring system (fully 3%; fairly 34%.) Of those companies with formal systems, just 9% ranked them as "very effective" and 71% saw their systems as "fairly effective." As further recognition of the importance of such information, 67% of the responding companies thought that their company's monitoring activities would increase over the next few years. That's probably what respondents to the earlier noted survey in 1959 also thought.

This apparent disconnect between believing that a system to gather, analyze and distribute information is important and the lack of progress demonstrated by the above surveys highlights two facts. First, U.S. managers had not become accustomed to functioning in a global economy. They remained focused on traditional markets, competitors and product life cycles which they believed they could follow on an ad hoc basis. Second, knowing you should do something and doing it often is the difference between excellent and bankrupt organizations.

I am reminded of a medical conference I attended. A physician was discussing the effects of age and lifestyle on the loss of bone density. He made the observation that the vast majority of his patients want to be tested too early and too often. If tests show any deterioration the patient expects to be given a pill to arrest and cure the situation. When he tries to discuss lifestyle changes, they simply want medication rather than taking responsibility/action for their health. They understand this is important, perhaps vital, but remain passive.

---

**Better managed organizations are those that rapidly pursue what they view as important. While it could be argued that General George Patton was predictable, the speed with which he struck made him virtually unstoppable.**

---

Collecting, analyzing and distributing competitive information does not require a large staff.

---

**Commitment should not be measured by the size of an organization, but its focus and effectiveness.**

---

## COMPETITOR INFORMATION SYSTEM
(Figure 1)

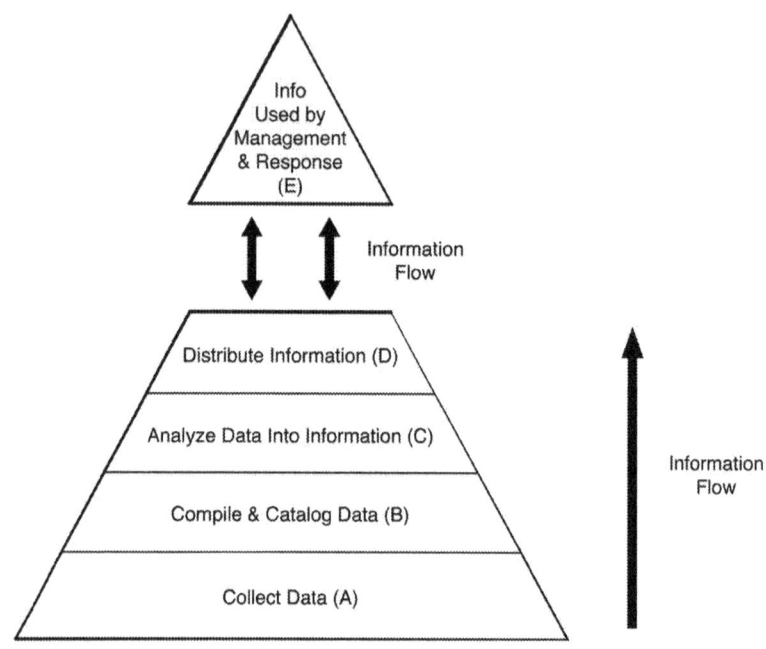

(A)   Collect data from internal and external sources. For example: internal sources - sales and technical personnel; external sources - annual and quarterly reports, websites, journals and newspapers.
(B)   Sort data; set up and maintain computer files.
(C)   Analyze data to provide information regarding recent competitor and market activities; competitors' current and anticipated market actions, financial position and production levels.
(D)   Routine and "as needed" distribution of information to management.
(E)   Management uses the information for decision making, communicates additional information needs and provides competitor data to be analyzed (Step C) it has gathered from its activities.

A small unit, perhaps one person, who as part of their activities are responsible to manage an information gathering and analyzing network, can perform all, or at least the lion's share, of this function. Additional support is readily available from external sources such as market research firms, etc. Companies usually discover that they have within their organization large amounts of competitor information once they alert their members to its importance and provide a system to manage it (Figure 1). The key is to recognize its importance and institutionalize a system to gather and process it.

---

**Competitor information must be seen as an asset to be contributed to and shared with other members of the organization.**

---

Organization Structure

An organization's structure must be designed based on its key activities. Several lessons have been learned as a result of the past recessions and increased global competition. Previously, as organizations grew, a disproportionately higher number of staff positions were added. These additions began for a number of reasons including technological advances, growth in the diversity of companies' products and markets, and increased government regulations. As a cost cutting measure, organizations have more recently reversed this trend by eliminating staff positions.

Too often organizations appear to have been caught by surprise by a downturn in the economy or their industry. This can result for several reasons. However, a natural bias to avoid unpleasant decisions as long as possible and hope things get better is usually at least part of the equation. As a manager it is often your responsibility to lead an organization in directions it would not go without you. This mandates that you overcome the inertia of the status quo.

---

**No organization is at a steady state; it is either improving or deteriorating, whether or not this is obvious at that moment. It is impossible to be at a steady state given constant changes in markets, costs (including laws and regulations) and competitors.**

---

When a surprise downturn occurs, cutbacks are not well planned and may not provide the intended benefits. In fact, without proper planning, large reductions can have the anticipated immediate negative effects without the offsetting increases in efficiency. Such actions may be rewarded in the short-term by senior managers or the equity markets, but this can merely be people confusing activity with progress. Also, the organization's survivors will be carefully watching how management treated those directly impacted by the decision, as well as the impact (increased workload, changes in benefits and pay, etc.) it has on them. Better managed organizations continually, through an identifiable system, act to increase efficiency, which includes flattening the overall organization structure.

Flatter organizations offer several advantages. Only a part, often a relatively small part, results from the reduced compensation cost. Fewer layers force management to be more selective regarding where they concentrate their efforts. This helps to focus on areas with the greatest payback and reduces or eliminates less important tasks. Also, the nonproductive efforts of "protecting or expanding one's empire" by adding staff are curtailed. By reducing staff and management layers, organizations are less likely to get caught up in a syndrome known as "paralysis from analysis," that is, to make excuses for delaying decisions far too long while analyzing "potential alternative actions."

---

**Flatter organizations place their members on notice that each is more visible and therefore must make decisions for which they will be accountable.**

---

Better managed organizations are prone to make decisions and flatter organizational structures can aid in the decision making process. Structure is further discussed in Chapter 5.

Defining Excellence

Since no individual or system can assure it will make the right decision at every moment, it is essential that an organization incorporate, as a visible part of its culture, a system where decisions are periodically tested and modified as necessary. There is a well known law of inertia in physics which states that a body will stay at rest or in uniform motion in the same straight line or direction unless acted upon by some external force. This law also applies to decision making.

---

**Once a decision is made, the activities initiated from this decision can take on a life of their own and be followed almost blindly to their conclusion, even if subsequent events have modified the desirability of that conclusion.**

---

In fact, poor long-term decisions can take considerable effort to modify since their early champions may, are likely to, attempt to protect the decision from continued scrutiny. In these instances, the original decision makers may feel threatened by changes and spend time hoping that future events will salvage their original decision rather than identifying the needed changes. Excellence demands that review processes enable management to overcome a poor decision's inertia.

The task of identifying truly excellent organizations is not easy. Therefore, a working definition of excellence may be helpful.

---

**A well managed organization knows, and outwardly shows, the importance of its members and information, does not lose sight of the basics in its business and industry, makes decisions based on its long-term view of the future and maintains a system whereby decisions are modified as events change.**

---

## References

1. Drucker, Peter F., "Management: Tasks, Responsibilities, Practices," (New York: Harper & Row, 1974), pp. 79-80.

2. Clifford, Donald K., Jr. and Cavanagh, Richard E., "The Winning Performance" (New York: Bantam Books, 1985).

   Collins, James C. and Porras, Jerry I., "Built to Last", (New York: HarperCollins, 1994).

   Peters, Thomas J. and Waterman, Robert H., "In Search of Excellence", (New York: Harper & Row, 1982).

   "America's Best Plants," Industry Week, annual survey.

   "America's Most Admired Corporations," Fortune, annual survey.

3. McGregor, Douglas, "The Professional Manager" (New York: McGraw-Hill Book Company, 1967), pp. 162-169.

4. Wall, Jerry L., "What the Competition Is Doing: Your Need to Know," Harvard Business Review, November-December 1974.

5. Sutton, Howard, "Competitive Intelligence," The Conference Board, Inc. 1988. While dated, this publication includes references to numerous sources of information in the area of competitive intelligence.

# CHAPTER 2
## PEOPLE, A MANAGER'S MOST DYNAMIC AND VITAL RESOURCE

Summary

Prior to going farther, we should focus on a manager's most valuable and dynamic resource, people. It is surprisingly recent that the importance of human relations in an organization's success has begun to be better understood. Later chapters discuss setting organizational goals and implementing plans to obtain them. This cannot be accomplished without the direct support of an organization's members. As we have seen, changes in the environment require a number of adjustments on the part of managers. Among these is an increased awareness of the importance of everyone's contribution to an organization. While various successful organizations can and do have systems with apparent noticeable differences, upon further analysis, there are important similarities at their core.

The importance placed on work and the reasons people work can and have often been overlooked.

---

**The job someone holds not only has a direct bearing on them while working, but also impacts their private lives.**

---

In addition to financial compensation, this includes an individual's view of herself and her acceptance by groups outside the workplace.

Historically, a considerable amount of effort has been focused on improving technology and maintaining production facilities, while less work has been done on improving the performance of those responsible for using this increased technology. As discussed earlier, one of the key traits of a better managed organization is that it understands the importance of people to its overall success and provides outward signs of this recognition. An understanding of human behavior is essential for effective management. People's behavior usually results from an interaction of their needs and the working environment management has provided.

---

**Good managers are trained, not born. An increased awareness of the factors affecting people's behavior can only result from a commitment by management.**

---

Managers cannot rely on some "common sense" beliefs regarding behavior. All too often these assumed truths prove to be inaccurate. Management can no longer satisfy itself with focusing on improving the returns of land, capital and equipment, while paying less attention to its most dynamic and vital resource, people. I recall an advertisement run by a company selling PCs some years ago. It showed a room set up with work stations and asked the question, "Which PC Is The Best?" The answer-"The One Your People USE."

Importance of Work

In recent years, people's jobs have taken on increased impor- tance. This should not come as a surprise, given the percentage of an individual's waking hours that are spent on the job, particularly if you include commuting and work related activities performed away from the workplace. Previously, it was expected that only those who needed to work for financial security held jobs. Today, even people who are financially independent are often viewed by others based on work related issues such as the organizations (including non- profit) they are associated with and their title.

Think about the first few questions you ask, or are asked, when introduced socially to a stranger. Usually, name is first, followed closely by "What do you do?". This simple, and admittedly unsci- entific, survey helps to highlight the importance of work in society. The increased emphasis on work magnifies the importance of all related activities, making it necessary that managers understand what people expect from their work, how they will respond to the actions of others, and the resulting role managers play.

It is vital that managers strive to build a basic understanding of what makes each of us behave the way we do. The research of Abraham H. Maslow and Fredrick Herzberg can provide insights into people's needs and the role the work environment plays in satisfying these needs. Like any behavioral theory(ies), their work outlines general tendencies. When coupled with an understanding of how people learn and form expectations, managers will have a basis for better understanding behavior.

Almost all behavior a manager sees in a workplace is logical based on the person's underlying assumptions. All too often, managers do not have sufficient background in behavioral theory and/or do not make the effort to understand the underlying reasons for an action.

---

**At times it is easier to label an action "irrational" than to try to understand it.**

---

Both when managing and teaching management, I have found it helpful to focus on behavioral/motivational theories by first trying to understand the needs of individuals and groups, and then on how the work environment can help in satisfying or frustrating these needs. At that point a manager, who is really only a practicing/ advanced student in this dynamic area, can better understand the impact of their actions. Two models of note are Maslow's Hierarchy of Needs and Herzberg's Motivation and Hygiene Model.

Hierarchy of Needs[1]

Abraham H. Maslow constructed a behavioral model based on a hierarchy of five levels of human needs. He believed that as a person satisfied their current need, the next one in the hierarchy became the motivating force. The lower level needs (physical, safety and security needs) are concerned with survival. Normally, physical needs are reasonably well satisfied in the workplace. However, the need for a safe, predictable environment (safety and security) can exert a strong motivating force on people, particularly given the often sudden and large scale reductions in the work force in many American companies.

The next two levels in the hierarchy (social and esteem needs) rely on interaction with others in the workplace. It is naive for a manager to think that social needs can be satisfied solely outside the workplace. The need for esteem and status requires a self-realization of one's worth and a belief that those around us perceive us as being of value.

Self-actualization is the need which is least visible since most people never work their way through the complete hierarchy so that it becomes the obvious motivator. It may be an important motivator, however, which can be attained by someone being able to perform their work while finding it challenging. To enable a person to satisfy this need requires management's attention to designing jobs, demonstrating their importance, and training the individual so she can successfully perform the tasks associated with the position.

Since not everyone moves through the entire hierarchy, rewards and punishments, to be effective, must address each person's or group's needs. This presents one of management's more difficult challenges. It should be understood that all needs do not have to, and are not likely to, be satisfied in the workplace. For example, busy people who still take time to do volunteer work. This obviously is meeting a need of theirs. In this case, it is important that the two separate groups (work and volunteer) are not in continuous conflict.

Although not normally used as a study in management, Dante's classic "Inferno" provides interesting insights into matching punishments to individuals. These views can also be extended to rewards. In this work Dante selected eternal punishments for people based on the way they lived. Punishments were directly related to the sin for which an individual was "damned." This assured that the people would suffer and know why they were punished. For example, according to Dante, people who committed suicide were deprived of their human form in Hell, while souls that were lost due to anger were sentenced to be in the waters of Styx beating each other for eternity. A soul's location in Hell was determined by the seriousness of the sin. The more serious the sin, the deeper in Hell, closer to the devil, a soul was placed, demonstrating that even damning behavior has degrees of seriousness.

**While in concept managers realize that a reward or punishment is only effective if the person receiving it feels rewarded or punished, the importance of this matching process is often not fully appreciated.**

Motivation and Hygiene Model[2]

While Maslow focused his attention on people's psychological needs, Fredrick Herzberg developed a behavioral model based on the role the work environment plays in attaining satisfaction for people. Herzberg postulated that the primary sources of favorable experiences while working were achievement, recognition, advancement, the work itself, and potential for growth/responsibility (corresponding to Maslow's higher level needs). He called these motivational factors. Unfavorable experiences appeared to be related to issues, such as company policy and administration, quality of supervision, relations with supervisors, peers and subordinates, pay, job security and working conditions. Herzberg called these hygiene or maintenance factors. It had previously been assumed that motivation and lack of motivation were opposites. Herzberg provided an alternative view, that the causes of satisfaction and dissatisfaction are separate from each other.

Fredrick Herzberg's model, as does Maslow's, outlines general tendencies. When dealing with people, there is no simplistic model which is 100% accurate. But these models do raise the question to management if its policies and practices are a match with the people they want to attract and retain. Do they act to motivate or demotivate employees?

**Herzberg's findings indicate that the only effective way to motivate people is to give them challenging work for which they are qualified, allow them to assume responsibility for the work and indicate some potential for growth and advancement.**

This is in contrast to relying on personnel policies, pay and fringe benefits to motivate. A major outgrowth of Herzberg's model is the concept of job enrichment/expansion and many of the so-called newer management concepts which stress increased involvement and authority/responsibility (empowerment). These practices strive to increase the motivational factors associated with performing a job.

23

As with any other theory, Maslow's and Herzberg's models have both supporters and critics. However, for a manager, Maslow provides a conceptual framework for understanding the needs of individuals and groups, while Herzberg's model directs management to a better understanding of the complex question of how to motivate people. Figure 2 attempts to show the relationship between these models.

**MOTIVATION THEORIES**
(Figure 2)

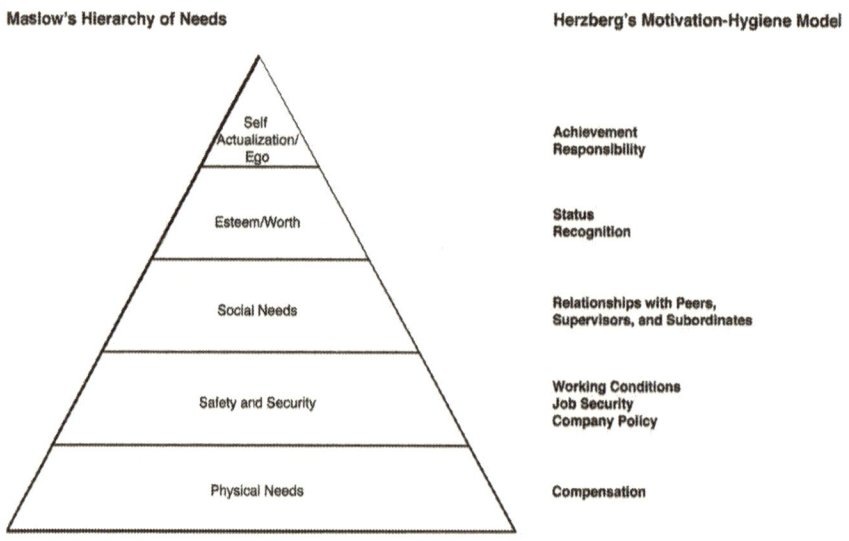

Maslow's Hierarchy of Needs

Herzberg's Motivation-Hygiene Model

Self Actualization/ Ego — Achievement / Responsibility

Esteem/Worth — Status / Recognition

Social Needs — Relationships with Peers, Supervisors, and Subordinates

Safety and Security — Working Conditions / Job Security / Company Policy

Physical Needs — Compensation

Maslow's theory concentrates on people's psychological needs while Herzberg focuses on the role the work environment plays in attaining satisfaction.

It is interesting that, in a survey by "Industry Week" about 63% of those responding (mostly middle managers and first-line supervisors) expressed a dissatisfaction with their jobs. The three main reasons cited for why their jobs were not fun are: "We're not a team" (49%), "The bureaucracy stifles initiative" (39%) and "My efforts are not acknowledged" (30%.)[3] Although care must be taken in interpreting such findings, they appear to be consistent with those of Maslow and Herzberg. The need to achieve and be recognized is essential. The stated dissatisfaction "with not being a team" could also result from a belief that efforts will not be recognized and/or a lack of clearly stated goals by management. While published in 1991, do you believe recent events would increase or decrease the average level of dissatisfaction?

You can argue that seeing a job as "fun" may not be necessary for an individual to perform required tasks. But, without enjoying work a person is unlikely to tap into their initiative and creativity. This leaves an organization increasingly relying on senior management's knowledge/ability to direct every effort. Obviously, this is not a realistic position, particularly in today's rapidly changing and competitive environment.

Rewards and Punishments

It is a manager's responsibility to link the needs of the organization with those of its members. The importance of rewards and punishments on behavior cannot be overstated. In his book, "Leadership Secrets of Attila the Hun," Wess Roberts points out, "Never underestimate the ability of the empire or other foes to gain the support and loyalty of Huns you fail to heed and rightfully reward,"[4] highlighting the need for people to feel that they are making a contribution which is recognized by management.

Douglas McGregor left us an outline for effectively applying punishments. His "Red Hot Stove Rule" compares touching a hot stove with a disciplinary action. Like the reaction we get from touching a hot stove, discipline needs to:

- Be immediate
- Provide warning
- Be consistent
- Be impersonal

These guidelines can also be used when rewarding behavior.

A reward or punishment must be applied as immediately as possible following a person's action so that the individual clearly sees the cause and effect relationship. It cannot be a surprise; that is, an individual must know what is expected and that an improper performance will be punished as an acceptable/good performance will be rewarded. It must be consistent to demonstrate that any individual or group performing that act will be treated in the same manner. Also, it must be impersonal so that the person understands that it is not management which is responsible for the reward or punishment, but the person, themself. Management's response is the result of someone's actions. For example, a student who scores an A on an exam should not thank the instructor for the grade, since the instructor only graded what the student gave her. The student might, however, thank the instructor for helping them understand the material. When giving a reward, how often do direct supervisors mention their role in securing it? When punishing, do they act the same, or at least partially blame others? The unidentified "they"!

The need to draw a direct relationship between the action and the results (reward or punishment) is clear. Let's revisit the classic example of a child and its parents. Assume a child misbehaved all day, and his mother, rather than punishing him at the time, threatened the child by saying, "Wait until your father comes home." During the day, the mother and father talk and she explains how the child misbehaved. In the evening when dad comes home, the child runs to greet him and is immediately met by a spanking. By failing to draw the relationship between the child's actions and the punishment, the parents have helped the child understand that he should avoid coming to see his father as he enters the house.

People need to know what is expected of them and management's likely response just as we know, in advance, what will happen if we touch a hot stove. This prior knowledge will help people to view management's actions as fair, as well as to establish a pattern of consistency.

---

**A disciplinary or rewarding action must be viewed by everyone as automatic based on their activities.**

---

Responses by management are not aimed at an individual but at an action. This increases the probability that members will view punishments as corrective and rewards as resulting from their good works. Many formal systems do not adequately provide an opportunity for management to clearly develop the relationship between an action and response.[5]

When used, particularly during difficult economic times, across-the-board actions place everyone into a single group. Such actions are intrinsically unfair, since they do not differentiate based on performance. It is safe to assume that any policy which treats everyone the same is generally unfair to better performers and may actually reward poorer ones. Although such actions are adopted for several reasons, they do not allow for the development of a relation between a person's work and management's action. In fact, if used for an extended period, they can foster an environment where better performers begin to lower their standards toward the average or leave the organization. Relationships as opposed to performance will become seen as the way to survive and succeed, giving rise to increased politicking and its harmful consequences.

Many organizations do not have a formal, continuous feedback system for employees. For example, under normal circumstances, performance or salary reviews are scheduled routinely, well in advance of any activity a person might perform. Therefore, it is extremely important that a manager stress, by using specific references, that the end result of such a periodic review is due to all actions performed by the person during the entire period. To make up for the built-in time lag of traditional systems, a manager needs to routinely recognize both positive and negative actions by people separately from any formal review system. As a rule, no one should be surprised by statements contained in a formal, periodic review. If they are, the supervisor needs to find a better way to communicate with them.

## Management - A Self-Fulfilling Prophecy

Based upon learning and experience, we form general opinions about people. Douglas McGregor identified characteristics of two managerial views, Theory X and Theory Y. These views directly influence behavior.

It is important to understand that Theory X and Theory Y are not strategies, but beliefs about people which influence management's actions. After reviewing a general list of assumptions underlying Theory X and Theory Y (Figure 3), it is easy to visualize these as opposite ends of a continuum. However, as Douglas McGregor pointed out, "Theory X and Theory Y are not polar opposites; they do not lie at extremes of a scale. They are simply different cosmologies." [6]

## UNDERLYING ASSUMPTIONS - THEORY X AND THEORY Y
### (Figure 3)

| Theory X | Theory Y |
|---|---|
| People avoid work. | Work is a natural activity. |
| Most people lack initiative and are lazy. | People possess initiative. |
| Employees are not interested in organizational goals. | People will accept organizational objectives if they help attain their goals. |
| Employees and organizational goals are in conflict. | Individual and organizational goals can be compatible. |
| People need to be managed by fear. | People respond to many influences, not just fear of punishment. |

If you believe the underlying assumptions of Theory X, you will behave in a manner which is likely to increase the probability that people working with you will begin to respond in a pattern consistent with Theory X. For example, if a manager believes people in general lack creativity and initiative, but introduces an "open door policy," he is unlikely to take the thoughts of others seriously unless they agree with his. This often leads to a series of occurrences where people express their ideas which are rejected, frequently in short order. New ideas, obviously, dry up. This ultimately lets the Theory X manager point to the lack of participation by employees as proof that people are lazy, lack initiative, and do not care about the organization's goals.

**The major error that a Theory X manager frequently makes is to forget that an open door policy cannot work with a closed mind.**

This is not to say that, if a manager holds Theory Y beliefs, people will always respond the way he would like them to and that rewards and punishments are not necessary. Theory Y includes the use of rewards for satisfactory actions and punishments for unsatisfactory actions. The Theory Y manager has available a larger selection of alternatives than does the Theory X manager. The Theory Y manager is not limited by his narrow view of people's natural abilities, indifference or assumed conflict with organizational goals. Therefore, he is much more likely to empower others which is the basic concept behind any management system to increase efficiency.

Theory Y proposes that people become indifferent to organizational needs and goals as a result of the organization's actions. A person's/group's prior experience under Theory X managers will make the task of a Theory Y manager even more difficult. In this case, the Theory Y manager must demonstrate that her views and those of the prior manager are different, and, therefore her expectations regarding participation are also very different. This requires a conscious effort by the Theory Y manager to continually stress the need for people's involvement by visibly noting examples of ideas which have changed the way the organization functions, and by carefully explaining why a rejected idea cannot be implemented. Be consistent, direct and a little patient. Don't expect perfection. Your behavior, which will be carefully watched, in different circumstances will be used to judge you.

---

**Remember, an idea is a very personal possession. Therefore, acceptance of an idea by management is often viewed as a personal triumph and rejection as a defeat.**

---

If people do not feel free to express their ideas, management has lost a valuable resource for improvement. Fear of having an idea rejected by management and/or co-workers is all too common, particularly during periods of cutbacks. This denies management an important source of problem solving, often when it is most needed. An awareness of this will help a manager in the delicate and necessary process of obtaining, evaluating and implementing or rejecting suggestions from others.

Before leaving this topic, for now, it must be stated that Theory Y is not a Utopian view of people. In fact, practicing Theory Y reminds me of a birthday card I once saw which stated, "Getting Old Is Not For Sissies." Theory Y requires you to invest more of yourself in the management process, with the accompanying higher level of expectations for others and the organization. Unfortunately, but predictably, people will disappoint you, at times to a degree that can make you question your basic approach or more. It has been said that "It's human nature to believe the best about others, which is why we tend to make so many mistakes with regard to people."[7]

However, for those who believe the basic assumptions and are willing to work to implement the concepts, it appears to provide a framework for organizational improvement.

Group Formation and Activities

Research, beginning with the Hawthorne experiment, shows us that it is normal for people to form groups in the workplace.[8] In fact, in our daily lives, we are members of a long list of groups ranging from small, informal social groups to large, formal ones.

Group formation in an organization cannot be ignored by managers since it is inevitable that groups will be formed and exert influence on their members.

---

**A manager who fails to understand the importance of group membership, or spends time fighting normal group formation, increases the probability that members will view the goals of the organization and those of the group as being incompatible.**

---

We all remember when our parents were concerned about the groups we joined as teenagers. They understood that groups place pressure on members to conform to certain rules or standards called norms. Members who do not adhere to these norms will be punished by the group, the ultimate punishment being expulsion. Members who adhere to the norms are rewarded. The active policing of members' activities by groups is essential for the group's survival. While perhaps more subtle, the influence of groups on their members does not disappear once we are beyond our teenage years.

Norms not only control the social relations within the group, but also, through those relating to production and behavior to outsiders, directly affect the attainment of an organization's goals. If a member over or under produces versus the group's production norm, they are punished by the other group members. At first, punishment can be subtle to inform the member that they are behaving inappropriately. This can even take the form of what would appear to non-members as good-natured jesting. If the member does not begin to conform to group norms, the punishment will be increasingly severe, including expulsion.

**Inherently groups are neither anti nor pro management. They are powerful, since they influence behavior of their members.**

While a group with low output norms (those below management's) will reduce output, groups with norms that are compatible to management's will help assure that the organization attains its goals. Therefore, the key to successfully managing group relations is that the goals of the organization and those of the group are viewed by group members as the same, or at least compatible.

Managing well defined groups is often easier than managing in the absence of these formal groups. Well defined groups have recognizable leaders with whom management can deal directly, as well as goals and norms which are more easily identifiable. The existence of groups does, however, complicate the process of introducing change in the workplace. While we all resist change, since we are giving up our normal activities in a known environment for the unknown, a group's resistance to change is increased because it may be life threatening to the group. Potentially, with change, some members may prosper while others suffer. Such trade-offs among members complicate relationships within the group and therefore are seen as undesirable.

Since group formation in the workplace is inevitable and will have such a significant impact on its members, managers need to understand the role groups play. As part of this, it is essential that managers recognize the goals and norms of the group and the way group members perceive those of the organization. As noted above, groups are not inherently anti or pro management. However, they are powerful and, by establishing a set of norms adhered to by a number of people, can magnify responses to management's actions.

Remember the above when planning changes. An early buy-in or, at least, acceptance by group representatives can create significant value by accelerating implementation. Explain situations/reasons for decisions, as much as reasonable and ask for assistance when possible.

# References

1. Maslow, Abraham H., "Motivation and Personality," (New York: Harper & Row, 1954).

2. Herzberg, Frederick, Mausner, Bernard and Snyderman, Barbara, "The Motivation to Work", 2nd ed. (New York: John Wiley & Sons, Inc. 1959).

   Herzberg, Frederick, "Work and the Nature of Man," (Cleveland: The World Publishing Company, 1966).

3. McClenahan, John S., "It's No Fun Working Here Anymore," Industry Week, March 4, 1991.

4. Roberts, Wess, "Leadership Secrets of Attila the Hun," (New York: Warner Books, Inc., 1987) p. 79.

5. The interested reader is encouraged to read works by Douglas McGregor and B. F. Skinner. Through their work they provide valuable insights into applying rewards and punishments and people's reactions to them.

6. McGregor, Douglas, "The Professional Manager," (New York: McGraw-Hill Book Company, 1967), p. 80.

7. Ringer, Robert J., "Getting What You Want," (New York: G.P. Putnam's Sons, 2000), p. 139.

8. Mayo, Elton, "The Human Problems of an Industrial Civilization," (Cambridge, MA: Harvard University Press, 1933).

   Roethlisberger, F.J. and Dickson, W.J., "Management and the Worker," (Cambridge, MA: Harvard University Press, 1939).

   Roethlisberger, F.J., "The Elusive Phenomena: An Autobiographical Account of My Work in the Field of Organizational Behavior at the Harvard Business School," (Cambridge, MA: Harvard University Press, 1977).

# CHAPTER 3
## PLANNING - DON'T RELY ON INSPIRATION

Summary

Planning is a disciplined process to identify current and future problems and opportunities, develop and implement solutions to the problems and strategies to exploit opportunities. Therefore, it is an integral part of a manager's role. Unlike the other three major roles of a manager (organizing, leading and controlling), planning is sometimes viewed as separate from a manager's normal ongoing responsibilities. This view will result in its failure since it is likely to be given a low priority or, worse yet, management can take on the passive characteristics of a spectator. Speed, in all facets of business, has always been important. Today's global economy makes it vital.

---

**Without preparation, acting or worse, reacting, rationally and quickly, especially in a large organization, is frequently impossible.**

---

In these instances, the decision process can become captive to one person or a product of infighting and/or emotion. An established planning system (culture) is the best safeguard against this. I am reminded of a quote I once heard years ago, attributed to Will Rogers: "Even if you're on the right track, you'll get run over if you just sit there."

**Planning requires a commitment by an organization to perform the necessary research and a willingness to take a critical (honest) view of itself.**

An environment must be established and maintained that provides for the internal communication and debate of potential strategies. Sufficient confidence in the process needs to be developed to allow management to implement strategies that may be different from the then prevalent conventional wisdom.

Planning is perhaps the most inclusive task a manager performs, since it not only requires an understanding of an organization's internal abilities and limits, but also of external factors such as markets, competitors, technology and future trends which will affect the organization's ability to compete. This chapter deals with the initial planning activities of information gathering and assimilation, market analysis and competitor awareness. Chapter 4 addresses the use of information and competitor knowledge in establishing an organization's mission, objectives and strategies.

Information - The Building Block

Obviously, when making a decision, the more inclusive the available information, the more likely we are to make better decisions and to feel more comfortable with them. As noted above, in order to form a strategy, management must have information not only about its own organization, but also the marketplace and its current and potential competitors. This requires a disciplined means to collect and evaluate data and to turn it into a product (information) which can be used for decision making. An outline of this process is shown in Chapter 1 (Figure 1).

The importance of information has long been recognized in many areas of human effort. Ancient armies looked for ways to infiltrate enemy lines and intercept messages in order to better understand their enemy's strengths and weaknesses. Sports teams, professional and amateur, have staffs which scout and analyze potential opponents. Although data and information collection and assimilation are basic to many human activities, its importance is not always recognized. If you don't believe this, remember one of the stated key benefits to forming the Department of Homeland Security was to better share information previously spread over several government agencies. It took a terrorist attack on U.S. soil to deal with this basic organizational problem.

All decisions begin with data/information, whether assumed or actually gathered and evaluated. Figure 4 demonstrates a basic model for strategy formulation and implementation. Two points should be noted regarding this model:

- Data collection and information preparation precede any decision and action.
- The process is continuous which requires further data evaluation, potential modifications to a plan and its implementation based on recent events.

## BASIC STRATEGY FORMULATION / IMPLEMENTATION MODEL

(Figure 4)

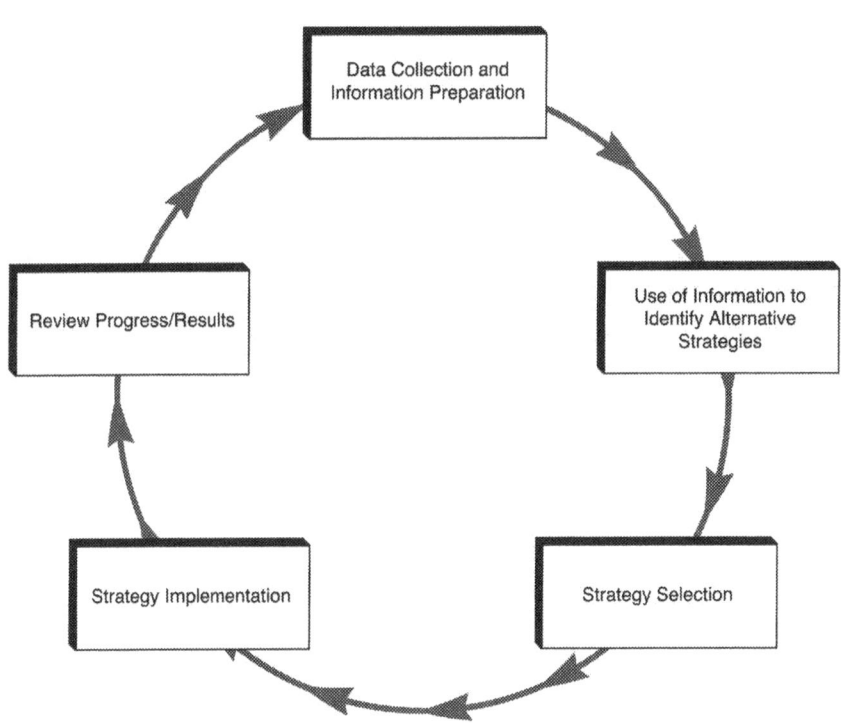

A considerable amount of data is readily available through published sources and normal contacts. Usually the difference between an organization which has adequate information to formulate successful plans, and those which do not, is a commitment by senior management to a process. Most experienced managers would probably agree that too often "the rigorous disciplines that management brings to the organization, transmittal and scrutiny of information about their company's internal operations...are noticeably lacking in the collection and review of available information about the external competitive environment."[1] This is probably as true today as it was twenty years ago when the statement was made.

Today managers are faced with an increased number of new, non-traditional, non-domestic competitors. With the exception of industries which require large up-front investments and lead times to enter, these competitors can appear with little warning. New entries typically begin competing on a cost basis, but as experience shows, they can quickly achieve a strong position based on quality. Despite numerous examples of this transition to quality, it continues to be overlooked by traditional producers. Just look at Hyundai's recent progress in the U.S.!

An effective data gathering and interpreting process does not require large additions of people and often can be accomplished with current staffing. For example, a salesperson making visits to current or potential customers may be able to get insights into that customer's inventory level and purchasing pattern, as well as competitors' pricing policies. If the salesperson keeps the information to himself, it minimizes the benefit the organization can gain from this asset. However, if such data is gathered, via a visit report, and provided to a central data base for accumulation and interpretation, the organization may increase its ability to make better operating and policy decisions. Advances in mobile technology provide the tools to make this and the entire intelligence gathering and sharing process efficient and timely, even on a global basis.

In an organization that encourages excessive internal rivalry and/or allows politicking to exist, it is rational for the salesperson to withhold information, especially if he had previously experienced and "survived" downsizing in the organization. Therefore, it is only by redefining the role of the salesperson that an organization can place itself in a better long-term competitive position.

**To be most effective, gathering and interpreting competitor data cannot be viewed as something to be done on occasion as the need arises.**

It is a continuous process which can only be effective if all the organization's members understand its importance. As noted by Michael Porter, "The data to make subtle judgements…usually comes in trickles rather than rivers and must be put together over a period of time to yield a comprehensive picture of the competitor's situation."[2] There are numerous sources of data which an organization can tap concerning both an industry or specific company (Figure 5). A little detective work can yield a surprising amount of data. This usually requires only a commitment by management and a willingness to assign resources including imagination to the process.[3]

Certainly, the establishment and management of a competitor analysis system is not without pitfalls. Among them is the potential for a lack of a clear understanding between those directly involved in performing the analysis and their internal customers (those using the information for decision making). The surest way to drain a system of its vitality is to produce a great deal of paperwork which is seen by others as irrelevant. To guard against this, a useful system must include participation by all levels of management (as shown in Figure 1) and incorporate periodic reviews to determine if the process is working. That is, is it relied upon when making decisions (?) and does it truly provide assistance (?) In short, does it meet the needs of its internal customers?

An honest review between individuals expending most of the effort providing the service (producers) and those relying on the system's output (consumers) will help to assure that the process is focused, seen as important, and accepted/used by management.

## TYPICAL DATA SOURCES
(Figure 5)

| Target | Sources |
|---|---|
| Specific Competitor Data | Company Reports, Normal Business Contacts (internal and external), Company Sponsored Media Releases, Trade Meetings and Journals, Employment Ads, Competitor Products, Website, Outside Services and Consultants |
| Macro Economic, Demographic and Industry Data | Government Reports, Periodic Reports and Conferences, Normal Business Contacts (internal and external), Trade Meetings and Journals, Outside Services and Consultants |

## Self-Evaluation

Thus far, we have been concerned with the importance of gathering data regarding competitors and refining it into decision making information. Before going further, we should discuss the need for every organization to look at itself. It is impossible to identify a workable, competitive strategy without a clear understanding of your organization. For a moment, think about an individual who is trying to plan a career. One of the key elements in this process is a self-evaluation to determine the individual's strengths, weaknesses, likes and dislikes. It is only after an honest evaluation is made that a review of alternatives can be undertaken.

Without a disciplined self-evaluation process, management can gradually fall into one of two extreme states of mind regarding their organization's ability:

1. That the organization is so superior that it will be successful in any business venture it undertakes.

2. That the organization has so many weaknesses that it cannot undertake any new business ventures and must avoid taking actions which might focus competitors' attention on it.

An organization which has enjoyed success in the recent past is more likely to adopt the first position, while a company currently experiencing difficult times may become depressed and fall into believing the second extreme statement. Although neither of these positions is likely to be true, belief in either will trap a company into making mistakes.

The super company image can lead to an overextension of financial, technical and managerial resources into ventures with low, or virtually no, chance of success. The loser image will ultimately stop an organization from undertaking viable economic ventures, as well as leading it to decisions which "give away" market share and profits to competitors. While these positions are obviously extremes, they demonstrate the importance of understanding your organization.

A thorough self-evaluation begins when management asks itself a few key "what questions" as discussed in Chapter 1. Key questions in a self-evaluation include:

- What do I bring to the market which is missing?
- What are my major assets?
- What are my key means to compete?
- What is my organization's track record in this or similar businesses?
- What is my financial position and commitment to this business?

Without a disciplined process to evaluate these and other related questions, it is easy to dismiss them in a superficial manner. Responses from a careless self-audit are typically general in nature and do not provide an organization with the insight to either run a current business or enter a new one. A poorly done evaluation often leaves management with a false sense of satisfaction or security since they have "done it." Therefore, going through the motions can be more dangerous than doing nothing. Figure 6 provides examples of incomplete responses to typical "what questions" based on a superficial self-evaluation and the information required for a more complete (valuable) evaluation. Ask the questions until you have clear answers!

Whether addressing a current business or potential new entry, it is vital that a self-evaluation be conducted. Other than the necessity for having a formal process for such an evaluation, there are few rules.

**Paramount in this evaluation is an understanding that senior management must be willing to accept the information which comes from a self-audit and either act within the identified limits of the organization or correct those limits.**

In recent years, it has become better understood that even the most successful organization may not be successful in every business venture. The move toward conglomerates in the 1960s and 1970s gave way to divestiture activities in the 1980s and 1990s by many of these organizations as they moved back to their core business(es). This often results from the realization that an organization has stretched its resources (management, finances, technology, etc.) too far. Management must be willing to accept that, while their organization's strengths will make some opportunities particularly attractive, its weaknesses will make other potential opportunities extremely risky.

Be honest with yourself and act upon the results from the evaluation process.

### INTERNAL EVALUATIONS - ASK THE QUESTIONS UNTIL YOU GET THE ANSWERS
(Figure 6)

| Question | Superficial Answer | Required Information |
| --- | --- | --- |
| What do I bring to the market which is missing? | Better product. | A product with higher perceived quality (list specific examples) at a lower final cost to consumers (give reasons for reduced costs, such as source of raw material, difference in production process, distribution channels, longer product life, etc.). |

| What are my key assets? | Better management, experience, desire to remain or enter the business and sufficient financial strength. | More experienced management (provide examples of management's track record in this and/or other businesses), strategic commitment (measure the importance to the organization of remaining in this business*), financial strength (funds available to this business and length of time the organization can sustain below par returns to improve its competitive position). |
|---|---|---|

*This can be done in a number of ways including: the percentage of the total organization's assets dedicated to this business, the relationship among this and other businesses in the portfolio, the background of senior managers, overall financial strength and the funds specifically available to this business venture.

Market Dynamics

A review of your organization's current markets or those it plans to enter is an integral part of the background work prior to establishing objectives and strategies. Markets are dynamic, and therefore are constantly in a state of change. Even if your organization has not changed any of its activities in the marketplace, the marketplace will be going through a series of changes. The typical Product Life Cycle graph traces the stages of a product from its introduction through market saturation and decline. Such a graph tends to make us think of this process as gradual, and one in which it is easy to identify the particular point in the cycle any product is currently at. Unfortunately, nothing could be farther from the truth.

Recognizing where a product is in its life cycle is not always easy. For example, the history of the home video game industry. This industry ran through the introduction and growth stages of the cycle very quickly, with the entry of new competitors into the marketplace throughout this period. As the market reached maturity, competitors dropped out and, within a relatively brief period, the market had hit saturation leading to strong price competition among the survivors. More recently improved technology has enabled the current players, including new entries, to move the primary battleground from price to quality. This established a new basis for competition, with added emphasis on visual quality, marketing/advertising and speed to market of new offerings. Even if you had survived the first wave of company exits, if you remained focused solely on costs your organization would have been gone shortly thereafter.

Despite the rapid initial growth followed by consolidation, a redefinition of the product, brought about by a quantum jump in technology, has given birth to a new version or an extension of the original industry. Today's video games have become a core part of the entertainment industry. More than half of American households have some version of a game machine.

Failure to identify where a product is located in its life cycle and when the battlefield has changed can lead to serious errors. If management believes a product is in its growth phase, when in reality it is in its early stages of maturity, management may elect to expand capacity and add personnel to met anticipated growth in demand. In such a case, the organization can spend funds through what should be the cash generating years of that product, thereby committing further resources in the false search of future growth. Conversely, if management is unable to identify a product's growth stage, it can freeze capacity and take actions to retrench its position, thus allowing current or new competitors to take market share. This process can be even more complicated in large diversified organizations that are likely to simultaneously have businesses and products throughout the various stages.

As a result of several factors, including changes in lifestyle/ consumer tastes, new businesses can result from a product which has hit maturity or even market saturation. Dress jeans and sport shoes are extensions of such mature products as blue jeans and sneakers. Also, dying product lines, or so-called ghost brands, can often be revitalized by a change of strategy ranging from pricing, merchandising, advertising, packaging and/or focusing on selected geographic areas.

Experiences regarding the supply/demand of energy over the past several decades provides a textbook case of market adjustments. As a result of the oil shocks in the 1970s, then current producers increased capacity while new producers were attracted to the industry. Consumers began to conserve energy, both through changes in their lifestyle and the increased efficiency of the new products they purchased. Caught up in the heat of the moment (which lasted years), public and private organizations began to look for more avant-garde ways to meet what was seen as a long-term energy shortage. This is occurring again. Potential solutions at that time included projects such as oil shale and wind power. However, before these new sources were commercialized, the expansive activities of suppliers from traditional energy sources and consumer conservation had begun to bring supply and demand back into equilibrium. In fact, even with outside actions such as Iraq's invasion of Kuwait in August of 1991, a position of oversupply of petroleum was reached and sustained. OPEC still regulates members' production.

A few basic factors caused this modification in the supply/demand relationship for energy. First, it had been forgotten that an identified resource, a product which was known to exist but could not be extracted profitably at current prices, becomes a reserve, a product which can be extracted profitably, if prices increase. Therefore, traditional sources of supply grew. The adaptab.ll of consumers and the expansion of production due to windfall profits acted to bring the market back into an equilibrium. These activities graphically illustrated what is meant by the old saying that each shortage sows the seeds of an oversupply and each oversupply those of the next shortage.[4]

---

**Remember, an analysis of a market is nothing more than a snapshot in time. Change will occur, whether you initiate it or not.**

---

Linking Competitive and Self-Awareness

Particularly due to the growing awareness of the global economy, the business community has turned a considerable amount of its attention to the topic of competitive analysis. Organizations have begun to realize the importance of identifying both current and future competitors. However, it is likely that only a relatively small portion of managers, who would tell you about the importance of identifying and knowing competitors, routinely conduct an analysis of these competitors. Again, saying is not necessarily doing.

A competitor is an organization or individual who provides a good or service into a segment of the market that you serve. This may be a comparable product to yours or a substitute. A potential competitor is any organization that can enter a sector of the market that you currently serve or plan to serve. One of the key points that sometimes is missed when looking at competitors, is that their organization competes with other individuals and organizations which have unique strengths and weaknesses like your own.

---

**Organizations do not compete against an entire coordinated group of companies. Furthermore, the quality of your competitors is more important than their number .**

---

While summary information regarding an industry is of value, it may not provide sufficient insight for selection of market segments or competitive actions highlighting how you can be most effective against current or potential competitors.

A competitor review must start with the identification of the market(s) your organization serves or is planning to serve. The question "What is a customer buying when he purchases my service or product?" must be continuously asked until you have a clear vision of the market. While this might appear obvious, organizations can fail to identify competitors and, therefore, make the wrong strategic move and lose opportunities.

For example, a bus company, with both long and short haul routes, which cuts the fare on its transcontinental route in order to gain a competitive advantage versus another bus company, has not identified its competitors. It is likely that, for a transcontinental route, its major competitors are airlines and not just an easily identified second bus line.

Automobile service stations compete in a number of market segments. In the area of automobile repairs, they compete with do-it-yourselfers, other service stations, chain stores focusing on selected auto services (oil change, etc.) and large general stores such as Sears. For gasoline sales, there are self-service stations and notably fewer full service stations. While you would expect some customers to be willing to move from a full service to a self-service station based on price, not all customers may be willing/able to do this. Therefore, a service station must address those areas it will choose to compete in and the means by which it will compete in each of the segments.

In looking for competitors of Rolls-Royce automobiles, it would be a mistake to limit your focus to other automobile manufacturers. The management of Rolls-Royce Motor Cars Ltd. long ago realized that their true competition is other uses of discretionary wealth such as a second home or art.

The growth in the number of stores renting videos or DVDs provides the consumer with the option of renting vs. buying movies and games. While this has expanded the market for these products, it has also likely reduced sales by the manufacturers. Manufacturers have fought back by lowering prices and expanding sales outlets. This, combined with the explosion of movies available directly on TV, has had a significant negative impact on renting. Markets are always changing.

While we could continue to list examples, all that is necessary is to reflect on the changes that took place in the commuter railroads. In some cases, it was not until years after their market had shifted from moving cargo, particularly mail, to moving people that the railroads understood they were no longer a cargo mover but a people mover. Therefore, while identifying your current competition seems easy, this part of the analysis should not be shortchanged.

---

**Management needs to return to the question "what is a customer buying when he purchases my service or product?" in order to broaden their understanding of the market segments they serve and to identify current and future competitors.**

---

The purpose of competitor analysis is to get a clear understanding of how your competitors are behaving currently, as well as how they may react to actions you take. Competitors may be a division of a larger organization. In this case, both the division and the parent organization need to be evaluated. As in any analysis, a thorough evaluation of every aspect of a competitor, while informative, may not be possible or even worthwhile. Therefore, it is important to focus on a few key areas which are likely to provide the greatest return on the resources used. If such an analysis indicates further work would be beneficial, it can then be done. The topics discussed in the remainder of this chapter are meant to help identify key areas for an initial competitor analysis.

## Competitive Analysis - Major Topics[5]

The increased competition from non-traditional sources has made it difficult, if not at times impossible, to attain data in all the areas discussed below. But I have never seen a situation where sufficient information was not available to at least reach useful initial conclusions.

An organization's financial resources are a key element in any evaluation. If your competitor is part of a larger organization, the financial strength of the parent company may become an indicator of potential competitiveness. While an organization with substantial untapped financial resources can be an extremely tough competitor, not too much should be made of this. It has become increasingly apparent that parent organizations with huge financial capabilities may not choose to subsidize divisions which are poor performers or, in the view of the parent, have questionable futures. It is important to look at the division as it compares to stated goals of the parent and its performance versus other divisions. A rich parent may not elect to carry a new venture which requires financial assistance unless it fits within the organization's other businesses or appears to have good long-term (time horizons are defined on a company-by-company basis) prospects.

The background of key managers, both on a division and parent organization level, can indicate how an organization views a particular business, as well as how it will compete and react to moves by others. An executive with a marketing background is likely to react differently to a competitor's challenge than one with a financial or operations background. Again, while such points may appear obvious, if they are not specifically addressed and put into context with other competitive information, their significance is frequently lost. In addition to the key decision makers, it is important to look at the next management level, not only because they influence decisions but they are likely to be future senior managers. If possible, discover the reasons managers have moved upward and, therefore, what activities current executives think are important. The manner in which an organization recruits its senior members (promotion from within versus bringing in from a different organization and/or industry) may indicate the depth of managerial

46

talent within the organization and the degree of confidence the Board of Directors has in management.

Compensation has been increasingly identified as a vital piece of information in competitor analysis. In the prior chapter, we discussed the importance of rewards and punishments on behavior. If this is important in managing people, and it is, it must be important in understanding the behavior of competitors.

---

**People do things for which they are rewarded and tend to avoid those activities for which they are punished. Therefore, an organization's compensation program plays an integral part in the decision making process.**

---

A compensation system which primarily focuses on current earnings will not only affect daily operating decisions but is also likely to influence other decisions, including the selection of a company's portfolio. A policy of buying quick earnings via acquisition can lead to purchasing earnings today, rather than building or improving existing businesses. This can result in buying fashionable businesses at high prices and may lead management to overextend a company's ability to finance and/or manage its operations.

Compensation systems in which the achievement of long-term goals is a significant factor will obviously direct a manager's efforts differently than one based on current EPS (Earnings Per Share). Since the compensation of senior managers has become an area of focus by shareholders in public corporations, more and more information regarding this topic is available through routine external company reports. As a result, an understanding of the significant parts of a competitor's compensation system may be more available than might initially be thought.

The appraisal of a competitor's commitment to a business is essential when formulating a strategy. Information regarding such a commitment can often be attained through statements by management, a history of the unit's importance to the overall organization, the status of the unit's managers within the parent company and the size of the asset base dedicated to this business. Obviously, an organization made up of one business will protect that business to a far greater degree than one in which a business unit makes up only a small, and perhaps not very profitable, piece of the entire organization. The concept of strategic fit may also be important when evaluating a competitor's commitment to a business. While it is not necessary that all business units fit a single operational or marketing scheme, the more interrelated a particular business is with the remainder of the organization, the more likely the parent will be to protect that business.

Over time, management usually develops an opinion of itself and its organization. It can view itself as a leader in an industry based on quality, price, technology or other major factors. It also might view itself as a limited competitor in select niches where it may attain acceptable returns without directly challenging major competitors. An understanding of a competitor's self-appraisal, as best as possible, provides valuable insight into the current and future strategies and retaliatory actions a competitor will take in a given set of circumstances.

An organization which is currently going through difficult times with one or more of its core businesses may not be willing to wage a strong competitive campaign, due to limited financial and/or managerial resources, against attacks in other business areas. While this organization may have previously been willing to fight to protect the business currently under attack, other threats to the overall organization may decrease its desire and/or ability to do so.

Although the concept of collecting and analyzing competitive information is not new, its importance has not always been appreciated by managers. During difficult economic periods, the pressures of the moment may act to distract management from activities aimed at better understanding its competitors. Both in the short and longer term, this can be a very costly mistake. Certainly, a brief review of military history highlights the importance such an activity can have in the final outcome of a major battle, or even a war.[6]

## References

1. Sammon, William L., Kurland, Mark A. and Spitalnic, Robert, "Business Competitor Intelligence," (New York: John Wiley & Sons, Inc., 1984), p. 23.

2. Porter, Michael E., "Competitive Strategy," (New York: The Free Press, 1980), p. 72

3. I recommend: Meyer, Herbert E., "Real-World Intelligence," (New York: Grove Weidenfeld, 1987).

4. For an interesting discussion of market dynamics, see: Drucker, Peter F., "Managing in Turbulent Times," (New York: Harper & Row, 1980), pp. 110-118.

5. For a more complete discussion and an expanded and somewhat different list of areas that can be included in a competitor analysis, see Porter, Michael E., "Competitive Strategy," (New York: The Free Press, 1980), pp. 51-56.

6. I recommend: Holland, Max, "When the Machine Stopped," (Massachusetts: Harvard Business School Press, 1989).

# CHAPTER 4
## MISSION, OBJECTIVES AND STRATEGIES - WHAT WILL WE BE WHEN WE GROW UP?

Summary

   Chapter 3 focused on the amount of effort required to prepare an organization to clarify its mission or purpose, establish objectives and select strategies consistent with the organization's mission. This chapter provides direction for using this background information in the development and review of strategies.

---

**Honesty about your organization's abilities and limitations and those of your competitors is critical in setting an organization's mission and developing and implementing strategies.**

---

   A strategy which is based on inaccurate information or desires, rather than facts, is doomed to failure. However, such a failure is unlikely to become immediately evident. An organization that follows a poor strategy can ultimately consume a great deal of management's attention, the organization's resources and lose market opportunities over an extended period prior to determining and/or admitting that it was the wrong strategy.

   While it is generally agreed that planning is a basic function of management, many managers have voiced disappointment with the results of their efforts. The problem may not be with the usefulness of planning, but with the nature of the planning systems employed. Actual systems can bear little or no resemblance to those described in management studies. I believe that it could be successfully argued that a great deal of management's disappointment regarding the results from their planning efforts is due to a misunderstanding of what planning is, and the role it should serve in the management process.

The idea that strategic planning can be done exclusively by a small number of people in a central group, or even in divisions, with limited contact to those responsible for implementing the selected strategies appears to be disappearing. The change in philosophy can be noted even by the reduced use of the term "strategic planning" and the increased use of phrases such as "strategic management." Unfortunately, it is likely that actual changes in management's behavior is far slower than in the literature. Becoming more inclusive and apparently surrendering some authority is normally a slow process.

A considerable amount has been written regarding establishing an organization's mission or purpose, objectives and strategy(ies). At times, descriptions given to each phase of the strategic management process can confuse the best students and the most seasoned practitioners. Therefore, it might be helpful to establish some simple definitions.

1. Mission or Purpose - An overall statement regarding the business(es) the organization is in or plans to enter. Helps define the manner in which the organization will be managed and compete in identified markets.

2. Objectives - Long or short-term goals. Establishes what is to be achieved and a timetable for its attainment.

3. Strategies - Provides a road map and timetable of activities to be implemented in order to attain identified objectives.

4. Operating Plans - A series of related, specific actions (tactics) designed to reach an organization's objectives. Implementation of an organization's strategy.

## Mission/Purpose - Where Are You Going?

The steps discussed in Chapter 3 of self-evaluation, market analysis and competitor awareness should result in an organization's ability to better define its mission and establish objectives and strategies to fulfill its vision of itself.

**If you don't know where you are going, any road will get you there.**

While I can't identify the original source of the above statement, I often use it to help clarify situations.

**BASIC ELEMENTS AND THEIR RELATIONSHIP**
**IN THE STRATEGIC MANAGEMENT PROCESS**

(Figure 7)

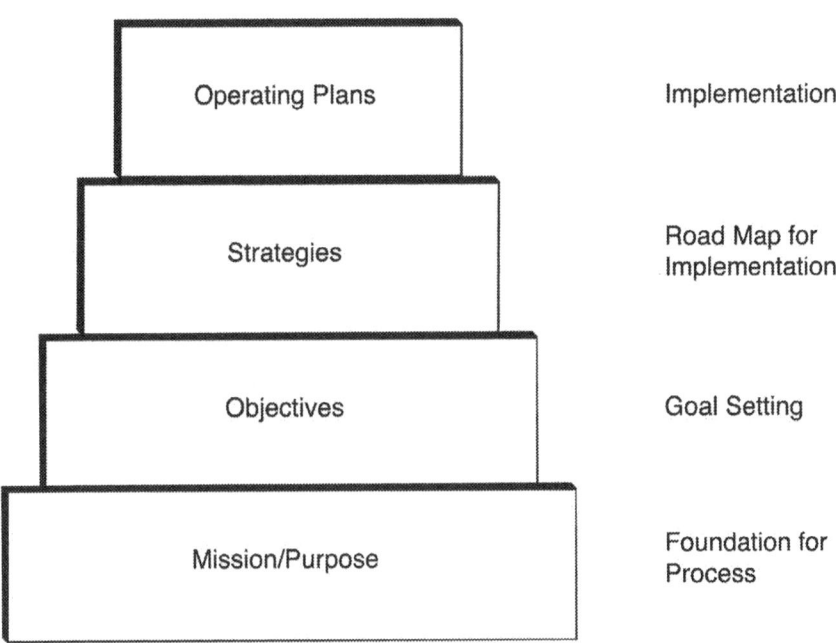

If an analysis results only in the collection of data, without playing an integral part in strategy formation, it is a waste of resources. An organization's mission should provide a long-term vision of management's view of what the organization will be. This includes the types of products to be produced and marketed, its geographic market and means of competition. It should also reflect the overall management philosophy of the organization, including such issues as its social responsibility. A mission establishes the scope of an organization's business, thereby focusing the resources of the organization. It is a type of "umbrella statement" under which the organization will conduct its business, both now and in the foreseeable future.

---

**An acronym all practitioners need to constantly remind themselves of is "KISS"; Keep It Simple, Stupid.**

---

As in most activities, simplicity can be essential to success. Just think of any team sport you may play or enjoy watching. In preparing for a game, the coach tries to introduce plays designed to confuse the opponent but to be understood by team members. In the area of missions, objectives and strategies, management's goal should be similar to that of a coach preparing for a game.

The role of an objective is to take the mission of an organization and break it down into concrete goals which can be measured. It is worth noting an obvious point - that an organization's mission and therefore its objectives can be expected to change over time. It is certainly not uncommon for organizations to change their scope of activities, either through diversification or via a retrenchment program. Therefore, mission statements and supporting objectives cannot be viewed as a constant. Reviewing and modifying them is necessary to successfully compete.

While modifications are to be expected, if an organization changes its basic mission and goals too often, say by chasing products/markets currently in vogue, it will assure failure. In such an instance, both insiders and customers learn not to trust management's apparent commitment to any business.

---

**Without dedicated people and a market which believes a company's management, an organization cannot survive.**

---

Trust requires a consistent and well communicated vision by management. Commitment is essential. One of the most frequently identified reasons for failure is a lack of commitment. This is normally manifested by a management that changes strategies (strategy du jour). Unfortunately, this behavior is often not recognized until the organization is in serious trouble.

An interesting exercise for managers and students is to review how companies describe themselves in public reports and in recapping recent significant activities. Reviewing Annual Reports and other published information for the last several years of a number of large organizations will show how they describe their mission, as well as the magnitude and number of modifications made to this view over time. This may provide insights into management's commitment to its stated strategy(ies)/programs as well as their reaction to changes in the environment. For managers, this exercise also helps to reflect upon your own organization and known and potential competitors.

Objectives

The process of setting objectives within an organization helps to insure that the organization will carry out its stated mission as well as to force management to review the reasonableness of that mission.

---

**By turning a global Mission Statement into specific objectives with an associated timetable, management is forced to review the probability of attaining these objectives in light of the environment and their available resources.**

---

Given normal limitations to resources (people, capital and technology), all objectives may not be achievable simultaneously. The development of a series of objectives forces management to set priorities, thereby focusing resources on the areas of greatest importance. It is worth spending extra time and effort insuring that an organization's objectives deal with both the internal and external environment and are specific enough to be measured, both regarding the results to be achieved and a timetable for their attainment.

For an objective to be valuable, it cannot represent a wish or desire nor can it be the result of an organization attaining its objectives. For example, a proposed objective for an organization that "it make money" could represent a desire or the result of it successfully carrying out plans. A statement such as "to make money" is not an actionable objective.

**Reported financial results such as earnings are due to past activities of that organization. Therefore, current results may only be valid as an historical measure of an organization's health. Be careful not to spend time looking through a rear view mirror.**

Attempting to build objectives focusing on the absolute size of such numbers may result in them being viewed as a causal factor rather than the result of a series of activities.

Objectives need to focus both on the near and long-term. Short-term objectives should be viewed as building blocks necessary to obtain the long-term goals. They provide both a yardstick to measure an organization's progress, as well as stressing the importance of taking action today to obtain long-term goals. Long-term objectives tend to focus on areas such as growth, market share, sales, efficiency, financial returns and technology.

For simplicity, think of the relation between long and short-term objectives in the context of planning a cross country driving trip, e.g. you were starting in New York City and driving to Los Angeles. Prior to the trip, you would establish a route, including the places you plan to stop and an estimate of when you will arrive at these points. In addition, you should set a budget for the trip including expenditures based on your progress. Your long-term objective is to arrive in Los Angeles at a specified time and for an estimated cost. The planned intermediate stops and associated budgeted expenses represent short-term objectives.

**To be effective, short-term objectives must be measurable events which directly relate to achieving long-term goals.**

These objectives inform management about its progress (time and costs) and provide a system to identify options if external (a road is closed) or internal (mechanical problems with your car) factors change and make your initial long-term objective undesirable or unrealistic.

Strategies

Mission Statements tell an organization what it wants to be, objectives establish goals consistent with an organization's mission and strategies provide a road map regarding how the organization will attain its objectives and therefore achieve its mission. Strategies put action into the strategic management process.

---

**A well conceived strategy directs the resources of an organization and provides a framework for day-to-day decision making.**

---

In small, single product, single market organizations, only one level of strategy may exist. The larger the organization, measured either in absolute size and/or the number of products and markets it competes in, the more likely the organization is to have several levels of strategy. Typically, two to three levels exist in medium to large size organizations.

Corporate strategy is concerned with running the entire organization. This includes identifying products and markets the organization will maintain, emphasize, enter or exit. Corporate strategies also address support services centrally provided to the organization, such as R&D, Human Resources, Finance, etc.

In some large organizations, several operations are grouped into a single unit. This is usually done based on similarity of production processes, products and/or markets. The strategies developed and pursued at such group levels address the means by which the organization competes in specific businesses and the allocation of resources among the group's businesses.

Farther down in the organizational structure, management is concerned with developing strategies dealing with the direct operations of a division or a Strategic Business Unit (SBU). These strategies are further refined into operating plans. Operating plans incorporate a series of tactics designed to assure that day-to-day activities are consistent with corporate, group and division/SBU strategies.

Therefore, a corporate strategy might include the selling of Business A and the use of the proceeds to expand market penetration of Business B. The group strategy containing Business A could include limiting capital expenditures to those absolutely necessary for the operation of the business and/or to dress up the business to attract potential buyers. The resulting operating plans would include specific actions to reduce costs and increase short-term earnings and cash flow.

Coordination of the levels of strategy is essential to an organization's success.

---

**The cardinal rule is to assure that management throughout the organization understands the overall goals of the company, their role and its importance to the organization's success.**

---

It is naive to believe that all details can or should be shared equally throughout the organization. However, it is even more naive to believe that without a general shared understanding of the role people in the company are playing, that management can efficiently employ their available resources. A shared view of goals helps to assure coordination of activities at various levels in the organization, as well as to provide a common framework for decisions. This encourages a broader, direct participation throughout the organization, thus applying a firm's greatest resource; its member's intelligence/know-how, and helps to achieve a sense of ownership in the company's programs. The following chapters discuss the need for shared information and goals to a greater extent.

Perhaps, in the vocabulary associated with planning and strategic management, no single word is more misused than strategy.

---

**Properly applied, the word strategy provides an organization with a road map as to where it is going and a means of attaining its goals. However, the word strategy can also be used as a defense for lack of action or inappropriate action.**

---

This can occur when management believes its current problems result from outside forces which are beyond their control, or when they continue to maintain a portfolio of businesses and strategies which had been successful in the past, but are clearly inappropriate for the future. Other actions which are sometimes justified by the word strategy include the lack of commitment when undertaking new ventures (this can be called reducing the risk), being seduced by high tech when an organization does not have the background or resources necessary to use or compete in this area, or taking on, in a head-to-head fashion, competitors in the belief (based on no real analysis) that you are better or stronger than they are.

In prior chapters, we discussed the importance of a thorough self-evaluation, as well as analysis of current and proposed markets and competitors. Without this understanding, management must rely on the insights and judgment of one or a few people to be continuously correct, outside forces to assist the organization, or employing some variation of strategies which are currently popular in the industry ("me too"). In the latter case, the organization has no advantage over its competitors and, in fact, finds itself following and copying others. Its only chance of success is to continually implement the selected strategy better than competitors who initiated it. A truly high risk position.

Increasingly management has become aware that, for strategic management to be successful, the process must include all levels of the organization and not only an individual or a small central group. "Planners" are becoming the chief coordinators of the levels of strategy and more and more of the planning role is being filled by senior managers responsible for the division or SBU.

Strategic management only works when it becomes an integral part of management's normal thinking process. In order to achieve this goal, the process must be viewed by all participants as having the support of senior management.

---

**One of the most difficult changes for some senior managers can be that they must view themselves as teachers and coaches and not the primary source of thinking and knowledge.**

---

Strategy Evaluation

It is not my intention to list a series of generic strategies which can be used as a starting point for selecting and implementing strategies depending upon the industry, your company's position vs. its competitors, etc. This has been done in numerous publications. But I would be remiss in not briefly discussing a means of evaluating strategies, as well as a simple exercise to help demonstrate alternative strategies.

As in most endeavors, the evaluation of a strategy can be simplified into answering a few basic questions:

• Is the strategy consistent both internally and with the outside environment?

• Is the strategy appropriate given your organization's available resources, risk profile and time horizon?

• Will it work?

While this checklist appears extremely simple, it can help to get to the heart of the issues which normally determine the success or failure of any strategy. Remember KISS! Answering the first question insures that management has done a thorough investigation of itself and the outside environment, including its current and potential competitors. This forces management to deal with issues ranging from its own strengths and limitations, to macroeconomic forecasts, changes in consumer preferences and technology. Getting by this part of the evaluation with anything more than just a glossy series of answers helps to insure that management has done its basic homework.

Every organization should understand the stakes of the game it is playing prior to implementing a strategy. Management must commit a certain amount of resources to the implementation of any strategy. Going forward with a strategy under the concept of "let's start and see what happens" without any specific commitment of resources, including time, is likely to result in a churning from one strategy to another, much like a gambler (vs. an investor) churns stocks in search of the quick kill. Strategies, particularly when building an organization, require resources, time, and have an inherent amount of risk. The difference between a successful implementation and a failure can often be credited to a company's commitment to a long-term goal and its willingness to absorb short-term disappointments in its pursuit.

---

**Just as you would not become a participant in a game without understanding the rules, management cannot afford to select and implement a strategy without committing resources (capital, facilities and management talent), accepting the risk associated with the strategy and providing sufficient time for the strategy to work.**

---

This is not to say, if it becomes clear that a strategy is not and will not work, that management stick to it. If this occurs, management must obviously modify its strategy or abandon it. However, without making an up-front commitment, it is likely that the first disappointment, not a failure, will be interpreted as a failure, attracting the attention of the corporate naysayers who will begin to bring pressure "to cut our losses." I have seen companies that encourage these naysayers as a means of so-called quality control or checking the strategy. This becomes a sad type of sport between those working to keep the organization focused and following the selected strategy and those who believe they are contributing by asking the most questions and disrupting the effort. This is likely to result in a situation of excessive internal warfare and paralysis especially when moving into new areas and/or technologies.

Prior to and throughout the implementation, every plan needs a last minute logic check. That is the purpose of the third question, "Will it work?" This provides an opportunity for management to review its strategy to insure that the assumptions it has used, both for its own actions and those of its competitors, appear reasonable and consistent with the environment, its knowledge of the industry and experience. While at times pulling back from a strategy, just prior to implementation, may be potentially embarrassing for selected members of management, it is obviously better for the overall organization and demonstrates the maturity of the decision making process.

### Grocery Shopping - A Review of Generic Strategies

A potential serious problem which can evolve for any management is a development of tunnel vision. People can become fixated upon their own industry and markets, not only in day-to-day decision making, but also in looking for models of strategic thinking. When this occurs, it is usually due to an evolutionary process, resulting from management's desire to learn all it can about its industry to become increasingly competitive. Therefore, while it comes from good intentions, it can severely limit management's view as to the possible strategies available to it.

---

**It is important for management to realize that strategic management is transferable, not only from companies in the same industry, but from companies in non-related industries.**

---

The more management scans the environment, including history, the more likely it is to find a strategy which can be adapted to its circumstances. This constant vigilance for insights into potential strategies has grown, and will continue to grow in importance due to increasing competition.

An exercise I have used for a number of years for both myself and students in strategic management is a periodic visit to the local supermarket. By walking around and observing the different

61

products and the way they compete, a manager in any industry can gain insight into potential generic strategies and even possibly a way in which they can be adapted to her particular situation. The following discussion is not meant to be all inclusive, but only to point out things that can be observed through a leisurely visit to a supermarket. The available lessons in strategy from such a visit range from being a cost leader for general commodity products to market segmentation and identification of new growth areas. Also be alert to potential lessons in production and distribution. Taiichi Ohno studied U.S. supermarkets in the late 1940's and 1950's in developing Toyota's Production System. Earlier, Henry Ford transferred his observations at a meat packing plant into the assembly line.

The beer and ice cream markets are prime examples of market segmentation. There are premium grades which compete on perceived quality, medium grades and lower/commodity entries for which price is all important. Cereal offers another lesson in market segmentation. The industry has been successful in developing large market segments. As a result, this potential commodity industry has a series of large specialty segments in such areas as health food and a children's market featuring new flavors and easily identifiable cartoon characters.

New products have come from changes in packaging rather than the products themselves. Examples of this include the packaging of detergents in washer load packets, as well as the packaging of coffee into a filter for use in an automatic coffee maker. In both of these cases, the inherent product has not changed, but value has been added by making the product easier to use.

An understanding regarding changes in socio/economic conditions and demographics is readily visible during a walk. The introduction of microwaves has led to an entire new market - microwave meals. Initially, only a relatively few choices were available. This has now grown to a significant market segment with constant product additions. Products in this area typically compete on availability, ease of use and taste. The rapid growth of markets such as health and diet foods is also obvious. Just think about the impact of the recent movement to low carb diets. A recognition of changes in our society to include single households and/or households where children often cook for themselves resulted in meals packed for individual servings. Again, adding value by ease of use.

As stated above, the examples noted are not meant to be inclusive, but only to provide a few easily identifiable examples of generic strategies which can be observed in such an everyday activity as grocery shopping. I have used this exercise for a number of years with students who are surprised at the amount they can learn from events in their everyday lives. I must admit that I have also found it helpful on more than one occasion. As competition continues to intensify, any process that helps a manager to expand her vision, and therefore awareness of significant events around her, will become increasingly important.

---

**Due to increased time demands, today's manager must learn from everyday occurrences and take these lessons and apply them.**

---

Training and experience needs to be supplemented by a curiosity about what has been and is happening in other industries. This not only allows a manager to increase his potential weapons (means of competition) but also to identify trends early which may directly impact his industry/business in the future. I have often told business students not to turn to the Business Section of the newspaper first, but to read the general global news. Frequently, the Business Section records and tries to explain what has happened, while clues to change are hidden in reports/discussions on non-business issues. Such issues have included proposed regulations and legislation, demographic trends (for example, increases in single parent households) and political events throughout the globe. Where were you more likely to get information which may have prepared you for the fall of Communism in Eastern Europe two decades ago, business or global news? How about today's clues for tomorrow?

Contingency Planning

To not at least briefly address contingency planning would imply that management can always anticipate future events, and select and implement a strategy to maximize the benefits or minimize the damage of these events. Clearly no organization can afford the luxury of assuming that the plans it makes today will be the best course of action forever. As noted previously, a manager must routinely review plans to insure that recent events have not modified the desirability of the strategies selected, or the means in which they are to be implemented.

---

**Contingency planning, like any planning activity, is nothing more than a disciplined process to help insure management focuses on the essential issues.**

---

While strategies are established and implemented based on expected events, occurrences with a smaller perceived probability of happening, but with a major impact on an organization, can occur. Contingency planning is the establishment, in advance, of strategies and operating plans to address these events.

There are only a few additional key elements to contingency planning. However, they can mean the difference between success and failure for the entire planning effort. The first is to establish an early warning system that points out when reality is different from the events anticipated in the organization's plans/strategies. This requires the selection of specific indicators, frequently referred to as trigger points, that identify the need to modify the organization's original activities and plans. Such trigger points can range from general indicators such as overall economic growth to tracing the impact on prices in a particular market based on actions by you or a competitor. It must be clear to all involved that the trigger points are measuring factors which are key to the success of the current strategy. This is an early warning system and infighting about the importance of changes in the trigger points after the fact can destroy the organization's ability to respond.

---

**As discussed earlier, decisions are subject to the law of inertia as well as the effects of naysayers. A recognized contingency process is designed to overcome these negative forces.**

---

The next step is to develop strategies and plans to improve your position based on these "less likely" events and a process by which the organization can formally modify its base plan. Such strategies and operating plans do not need to be as detailed as those contained in your base plan, since their purpose is to help you respond quickly to events which are seen as less probable. Therefore, alternative strategies and tactics need only be developed to a point to enable a rapid response to such events.

Management, which chooses to develop alternative plans to the same degree as its base plan, runs the risk of creating an attitude of indifference towards strategic thinking, as the process appears to be a massive paper exercise. Contingency planning is a vehicle to insure that management is not caught by surprise, but if carried to an extreme, it can cause paralysis and indifference.

## References

The strategy process and a review of generic strategies can be found in numerous works. Prominent among them are two by Michael E. Porter: "Competitive Strategy" (1980) and "Competitive Advantage" (1985), both published by The Free Press, (New York).

Books that help demonstrate the need, successes and failures of strategies include:

Byrne, John A. and Welch, John F., Jr., "Jack Straight From The Gut", (New York: Warner Books, Inc., 2001).

Collins, James C., "Good To Great", (New York: HarperCollins, 2001).

Holland, Max, "When the Machine Stopped", (Massachusetts: Harvard Business School Press, 1989).

Maynard, Micheline, "The End Of Detroit", (New York: Doubleday, 2003).

# CHAPTER 5
## STRUCTURE - DOING

Summary

The best plans can have disastrous results if poorly implemented, and proper organizational structure is essential for effective implementation. While this is agreed to by all, its significance is also easy to overlook. Considerable time could be spent discussing the pros and cons of centralized versus decentralized, as well as such examples as functional, product, territorial and customer-centered structures. This has been done in countless publications. A listing or brief description of known structural options can miss the key starting point for any discussion about organizational structure. That is, no single structure is correct for all organizations, even those thought to be in the same business.

**Structure must be driven by the business and its strategies since this is the vehicle through which the organization implements strategy to obtain its goals.**

Therefore, an organization's structure should be based on the significant activities of the business(es), with periodic reviews as the business(es) and the environment change.

**Structure aims to provide two sometimes conflicting attributes - focus and flexibility.**

The structure of an organization is too important to simply rely on an evolutionary process. It is naive to think that any organization, particularly a large international one, can radically modify its structure to meet changes in its business(es) quickly and provide a structure capable of meeting its new needs through evolution. It is only through an understanding of the business(es), their required activities and a clear view of an organization's mission and goals that an efficient structure can be achieved. Periodic organizational audits can provide valuable insights into needed changes which can obtain/maintain a competitive advantage for an organization. Evolution does not respond quickly enough to change and can be reliant upon the beliefs of a few people, as compared to a formal process of planning and reviewing an organization's structure based on its current and anticipated activities. Dinosaurs relied on evolution!

Structural Clarity

---

**It can be expected that the amount of time and effort spent in activities commonly referred to as politicking are inversely related to the strength and clarity of an organization's structure.**

---

Activities such as "empire building" and "protecting yourself" from various power groups within an organization are not only a waste of time, and therefore resources, but can also be destructive. For an organization to successfully implement plans and attain its goals, a clear structure must exist in which people understand their own, as well as others' authority and responsibility.

As discussed earlier, well managed organizations design structures to address their current business(es) and provide a system in which these structures can be changed as business activities are modified. This reduces the amount of time and resources consumed by individuals to protect their current positions or increase their influence. These self-centered activities can result in excessive staff and other costs but, probably more importantly, interfere with an efficient decision making process as groups tend to jockey for a position where they will be credited with success but insulated from failure.[1]

An ambiguous organization structure can unintentionally provide an environment where risks, and therefore opportunities, are avoided as opposed to one in which risks are identified and managed in order to improve an organization's overall returns.

A clear structure provides mechanisms to alleviate normal conflict within an organization. Probably the single most common source of conflict results from competition for scarce resources. Just like in our personal lives, wants/desires can often exceed our resources. In order to deal with this, most individuals use some kind of a budget for their personal expenditures. Organizations must also learn to deal with this and other routine sources of conflict. When handled constructively, competition for funds and/or people can be positive since it provides an opportunity for an organization, as a whole, to review a number of potential plans and focus the resources of the organization. But, without a strong organizational structure, such activities can become "threatening" to individuals and therefore destructive rather than a positive influence.

A well understood structure also encourages open discussions by all parties to resolve problems. This interchange of ideas can provide senior management with different views regarding the resolution of current or anticipated problems or pursuit of opportunities. Although an exchange of ideas by people with the same goal and different backgrounds is of obvious value, it will only take place in an open/positive manner if the organization's structure is sufficiently clear as to offer a channel for it, as well as protection and encouragement for those participating. How often do parents "argue" over how to raise a child, particularly the first? Both parents have the same goal - what's best for the child. However, different backgrounds can give rise to lively discussions. In the end, isn't that best for the child?

In a poorly defined organization, individual or group views are likely to be debated at various points in the organization without ever reaching the company's senior decision makers, or provided to them only in closed meetings with the intention of gaining support for a personal idea.

Such "politicking" is destructive to an organization and does not provide decision makers with alternatives for solving problems or recognizing opportunities, since the information is normally provided to them in a series of impromptu meetings and without the benefit of those with a different view. Therefore, they are given a series of views, over a period of time, by individuals or small groups, without the opportunity to compare the potential outcome of these positions with others, or possibly select the best parts of each.

**Politics is not only destructive, because of the impact it has on individuals and the time and resources it consumes, but more importantly, it hampers the decision making process.**

A clear, strong organizational structure is the best deterrent to this activity, and will stop potential debates regarding authority and responsibility. When designing an organizational structure, whether for an entire company or a department, it is helpful to view the potential life of the organization as infinite. This will highlight the need for a durable and adaptable structure.

**In addition, by viewing the potential life of an organization as infinite, it focuses attention on the probability that, over the life of the organization, every position is likely to be held, at some point, by a person who is not fully prepared to hold it.**

The structure must be strong enough to withstand having possibly several people, throughout an organization, hold positions, at a given time, that they are not prepared to fill. Such a view is not pessimistic but merely recognizes normal probabilities. An individual need not be a student of organizations, public and/or private, to recognize this and want to insulate her organization.

Design for Simplicity, Focus and Change

Structure is driven by a company's strategy and direction, as well as its current and anticipated portfolio of assets. Therefore, there must be a clear vision where management intends to lead the organization, as well as the current requirements for managing the existing portfolio.

---

**Strategy drives structure. Without a clear vision and strategy, selecting the proper structure is a hit or miss proposition.**

---

As discussed in Chapter 2, better managed organizations tend to have certain common characteristics. Among them is a shared purpose or direction. By having a clear, well communicated direction, the best structure for an organization will also become clear.

If it is intended to significantly change the business' portfolio, management may decide to use a temporary structure, with a planned series of modifications over time. In fact, every organizational design must accommodate change. For example, as companies acquire or divest business units, their structure needs to be able to respond. Also, as business units go through different phases of the life cycle, the key tasks required to manage them will change. Therefore, the structure required to perform these tasks must respond to the needs of the business(es).

---

**Management which focuses largely on today's activities without a direction of where they are leading the organization will wind up continually modifying its structure on an ad hoc basis. This can lead to confusion on the part of its members, increase people's anxiety relating to their job responsibilities and careers, as well as increase the probability that the necessary resources to manage the business(es) are not delivered in an efficient manner.**

---

Commitment and Resources

There are several signs which usually demonstrate management's commitment to a business. These can include the company's name, the way it presents itself to members and outsiders, and its structure. Since the purpose of structure is to help perform the important tasks for running an organization, structure should provide a clear indication to observers of management's direction and its commitment to each business unit.

For example, a structure which links the entire company with an identified business unit by sharing resources, staff, etc. is a clear indication of management's commitment. Conversely, establishing a business unit, separate from the core activities of the company and without clear linkage to that organization or a unique, well communicated charter, may represent a decision by management to exit.

**Either consciously or unconsciously, structure will ultimately show management's plans or visions for the organization and its beliefs as to the importance of units/functions in that organization.**

It would be a serious mistake to believe that even the "best" organizational structure will succeed if it is starved from necessary resources.

**The necessary resources for an organization go beyond those normally thought of such as money. They include time, as well as the commitment of competent people and training.**

Structure must provide an opportunity to enable valid ideas to be tried, even if initial results do not meet early expectations, and retried as long as the idea appears to hold realistic expectations of success. We all are familiar with the slogans regarding perspiration not inspiration being the basis for success and the old adage, "If at first you don't succeed, try, try again." A structure which fails to demonstrate management's commitment to a new idea makes it increasingly difficult for a manager to "stick to it" since he will often find himself defending the idea to onlookers and naysayers.

Structure - A Delivery System

When establishing or reviewing an organization, it may be helpful to think of its structure as a large delivery system for goods and services which begins from within the organization (internal customers) and ultimately leads to external customers. In the past, competitive advantage was gained by technology. In the future, speed is likely to be a major source of competitive advantage in designing and manufacturing new products, as well as delivering them in a timely manner to consumers. One of Corporate America's acknowledged weaknesses has been its inability to develop new, consumer driven products and get them to the market quickly. As "just in time" systems grow, the organization which can repeatedly deliver a quality product quickly will build a major competitive

72

advantage vs. its current competition, as well as a barrier to entry against potential new competitors.

---

**Technology can be acquired or copied by competitors, but a culture that simplifies communications and increases speed can take years to acquire, if at all. This is a real competitive edge.**

---

For example, many organizations have attempted to copy the Toyota Production System drawing upon numerous sources of information including: visits to Toyota plants, literature by people with first-hand experience and consultants. Even those having made measurable progress would admit they are still students and the implementation was more difficult and early results bumpier than anticipated. [2] Successfully incorporating such a culture provides the organization with the most powerful competitive position: increasing overall quality and decreasing costs by a means which cannot easily be copied. Structure is a vital part in developing and maintaining this position. More on the required ingredients to follow.

Given the acknowledged need for speed as a means of competition in the future, a considerable amount has been written about generic structures such as flat vs. tall organizations. Let's start here. A flat organization has some obvious advantages including:

- Shortening the lines of communication.
- Decreasing the amount of time required for decisions.
- Engaging more people in decision making.
- Reducing the potential for politicking.

The only advantage a tall structure would appear to have is to insure that routine functions are accomplished in a prescribed manner, with a high degree of control.

I have found it helpful when discussing organizational structure to not only look at "the height of the organization" but a number of other factors. Figure 8 shows a typical or traditional diagram of an organizational structure, as well as an alternate way of thinking about structure. The alternative view links the parts of the structure together with chains rather than solid lines. In addition, the customer, the only reason for a business to exist, is recognized. Often, organizational diagrams do not include the customer, but stop at the highest level of management or the ultimate owners, the shareholders. Without the customer, the business would not exist. In fact, it is increasingly important to actively include customers when designing, producing and marketing existing or new products.

The use of solid lines in drawing an organization's communication channels may, unintentionally, leave both the architect and the reader with some misunderstandings of the way organizations really function. For example, a solid straight line indicates that communications are always over the most direct path and that the organization is of equal strength over its entire structure. When was the last time you saw an organizational chart drawn which included a kink in one of the communication lines?

By using a chain to show relationships/flow, several possible problems come to mind. These include:

- The possibility that slack exists in the chain due to a poor design, excessive procedures or the behavior of individuals.
- A weak link may exist, which can be taken out, thereby shortening the process and making it more effective.
- The chain might be too tight, that is, the organization may have been shrunk down too far and resources are being stretched beyond their true capabilities.

Also included in this alternative view are horizontal communication links. These paths exist in every organization but are not typically shown.

The addition of the customer in the organization chart is vital. Companies continue to find themselves in situations where significant costs are incurred during design and start up of new products which prove to be unsuccessful since they do not satisfy a real need. Also, firms continue to lose business due to delays in providing goods and/or services vs. competitors. The cost of not being first to market has always existed, but with expanded global competition and shorter product life cycles the cost has greatly increased, and in a growing number of instances it can be life threatening.

---

**You cannot blame a customer for going to another organization to satisfy her needs if you don't. That is exactly what you would expect an educated consumer to do in a global market.**

---

74

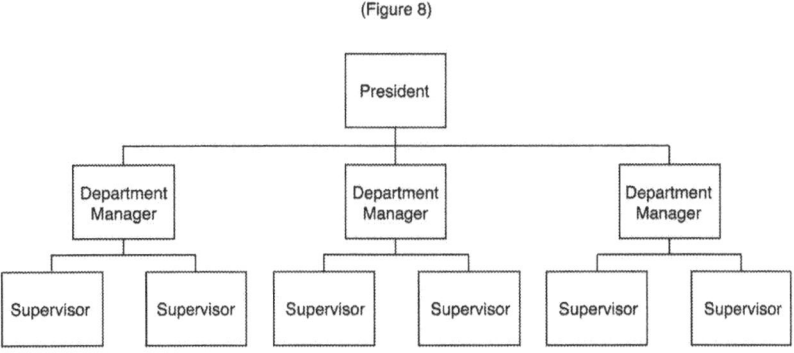

**TRADITIONAL ORGANIZATIONAL VIEW**

(Figure 8)

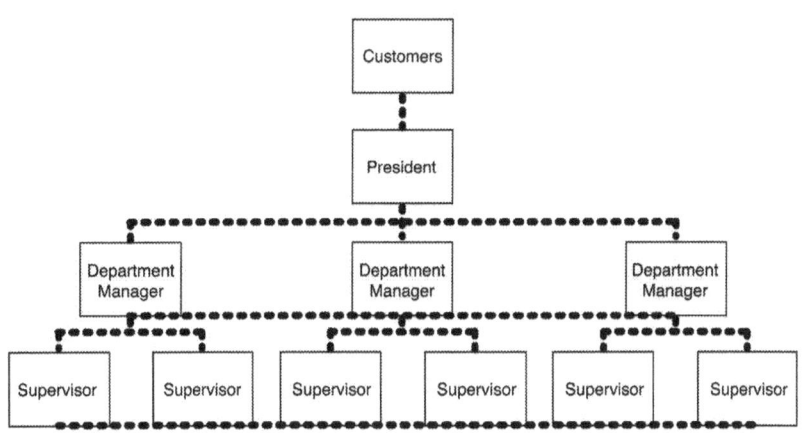

**ALTERNATIVE - CUSTOMER DRIVEN / GOAL SHARING VIEW**

Organizations can't afford to make products which satisfy historic needs and/or needs management believes exist. The only way to insure that this doesn't occur is to set up an active line of communications with a cross section of your customers and be willing to respond to the information you receive from them, rather than insisting that "we change their view" because it is more convenient for us.

As I write this, I am reminded of reports following Operation Desert Storm describing how some American companies lost potential business for the rebuilding of Kuwait. This happened despite being asked to bid. In fact they were considered the favored vendors. However, their delivery times were measured in weeks to a month vs. competitors from other nations that were measured in days. Remember, this happened at a time when we were entering a recession and therefore demand for industrial goods in the United States was relatively flat and falling.

"The Customer is King" cannot only be a popular slogan but must be a way of life for an organization to survive. This is not possible if the structure the organization chooses is outmoded and does not focus attention on the customer, the most rapid/efficient way of satisfying him, and a means to empower people to directly participate in achieving the goals of an organization. Perhaps no one in recent times understood this better than the late Sam Walton.[3]

The ideal situation is to have one-to-one (direct) relationships throughout, with the production/delivery process (good or service) being determined by the customer, whether internal or external. This Pull System (customer needs set the production/delivery process) assures that what is required is made, reducing waste. Go back to our supermarket visit in Chapter 4. Customer demand dictates the restocking schedule. With this vision, items previously thought of as assets such as inventory may really be slack in the chain (waste). If your customers have a goal of "just in time", why shouldn't you?

Having received my initial training in production management decades ago, I was accustomed to view process flows starting with raw material input. Years later I began, upon someone's advice, to start reviews at the point of product delivery to the ultimate customer and go back to the start of the process. The customer must be the focal point of the delivery system. How obvious, but how often overlooked!

Ask The Customer

The technique that I have used many times to remind myself, and those who work with me, of the importance of the customer is to establish an open and non-threatening line of communication with the customer using informal surroundings. Frequently this takes the form of a periodic lunch, which is stated to have no real business reason, during which time either I or the individual responsible for the account asks the question, "Since our last conversation, what have we done that has made your life difficult?" At first this takes the customer by complete surprise since it is apparently unusual to openly ask for complaints. This is particularly true if a senior manager is present. However, with time, such an informal gathering can provide the type of environment where your customer will begin to be honest with you, once he sees that it does not cause a problem in your organization, and that you respond to comments. For this to work, those present must clearly demonstrate that the customer's answer is not a threat to anyone in either organization, but a sincere effort to understand his needs and how you are or are not meeting them.

Do not expect instantaneous results from this type of process, since it will take time to build mutual trust. The required time will depend on the corporate culture of your customer, as well as their personal comfort with such open communications. Over time, your customer will tell you things that you must know and frequently it will stop him from going to a competitor.

---

**If you respond to his needs, the customer has a choice of working with a proven, responsive partner or trying to start up a new relationship with your competitor.**

---

In almost every case, the latter introduces considerably more risk and a greater investment of time than the customer is willing to make, therefore setting up a strong barrier to entry vs. your competitors.

---

**Customers know more about the value of your product than you do.**

---

In this case, "The Customer Is Always Right." How is a price set by a producer of a good or service? Typically it starts off based on the cost to produce and management's perception of the market. Is the value a product delivers to the user necessarily correlated to your cost? NO - you may be inefficient or extremely efficient, and your product may contain values or costs to the user which are not obvious to you. In a perfect world, a product's price would be based on value delivered. Ultimately, a non-economic product is replaced in the market. But that is an expensive way to learn!

The best and perhaps only way to realistically estimate the value of your product is through contact with customers. How else can you learn how your product is used, what happens (good and bad), and the potential problems your customers may be facing?

A growing number of companies use outside consultants to interview major customers, to provide a profile of how they are perceived in the marketplace. This tends to remove the initial threatening relationship between the customer and yourself, since no single customer is identified with a specific response, and it provides a fairly quick market profile of your organization. This is only a first step in building a long-term "partnering" relationship.

---

**Ultimately, direct contact is vital to foster trust and an exchange of information/perceptions.**

---

I believe the reason more senior managers do not participate in a direct relationship is that it is uncomfortable. It is extremely uncomfortable for a senior manager to sit and listen to a customer's problems with his organization and not to overreact either in defense of his organization or to attack/blame someone. The more senior the manager, the more uncomfortable they sometimes appear when placed in these situations. While you expect that problems with those you service or get services from internally (internal customers and suppliers) would be resolved quickly on a one-to-one basis, here too, a non-threatening, informal follow-up process is a good idea.

It must be remembered that the above process is not an exercise in placing blame, but one in understanding each other and exposing yourself more fully to the customer and them to you. Management, to be effective, must be visible in a business environment, not only internally but externally.

I recognize the above practice appears aimed at a business with a limited number of large external customers. This approach, with modification, can be used for internal customers and for a business with many small external customers. For example, focus groups are a standard vehicle to have direct contact with customers. What about Comment Boxes, walking through your place of business to speak with customers, or making visits to customers, even small ones? All these can and do work if you respond to the information gained.

## Ventures - Growth Outside the Standard Organization

After some consideration, I decided to include a section in this chapter concerning venturing. To date, many large organizations desiring to enter new businesses, with little or no prior experience, have experimented, often with disappointing results, while others have shied away from potential opportunities due to uncertainties. If an approach could be developed to help unite large and small organizations, Corporate America would greatly benefit. Outlined below is simply one approach to forming a bond between large and small companies with the potential to last beyond the initial emotional rush which is common at the onset of any union.

Much like capital leases have been referred to as "off balance sheet financing," ventures can be called "outside growth vehicles." In forming relationships with other organizations, companies seek to exploit their strengths and correct their weaknesses. A major challenge for management is to maintain an organization's clear structure while retaining flexibility to foster growth in new areas.

## Experience in Uniting Organizations

Corporate America has extensive experience in merging with or acquiring firms. However, its track record of being able to unify an acquired firm with the acquirer and provide a single organization with increased growth potential has been somewhat shaky. All too often, major portions or all of an acquired company are resold several years after the acquisition. It is worth remembering that frequently the acquired company is relatively the same size as the acquirer and in similar or related businesses. Also, the acquiring company usually has a significant body of data regarding the target organization prior to the acquisition. Looking at this track record highlights the difficulty of:

- Incorporating a small, unrelated start-up venture into a large organization; or
- Forming a partnership between a large, publicly owned corporation and a significantly smaller, often private, company.

The obvious cultural and structural differences between such organizations make a marriage extremely risky. Small venture organizations are usually in higher risk businesses and lack resources for development. If successful, these companies often do not have sufficient management talent/experience, or other

79

resources, to fully exploit their potential markets. Conversely, large organizations are typically set up in a hierarchical structure which is designed with a number of objectives, including the protection of its current assets and businesses.

---

**The existing culture in large hierarchical structures has, as one of its objectives, the continuation of much of the status quo while smaller/venture companies are dedicated to change.**

---

Large organizations, however, have resources which can be vital in the development of a new idea (money, facilities and experience), as well as an ability to produce and market products (Figure 9).

In recent years, advances in technology and lifestyle changes have shortened product life cycles at record speed. This has increased the need to provide an organization with a flow of ideas with an acceptable chance of being developed into products, and the ability to quickly commercialize these ideas. Therefore, a formula for successful marriages between these unlikely, but potentially synergistic, partners has been sought by practitioners and academicians alike.

## SEARCHING FOR SYNERGIES
### (Figure 9)

|  | START-UPS/ VENTURES | LARGE ORGANIZATIONS |
|---|---|---|
| **Structure** | Informal - can appear chaotic. | Hierarchical. |
| **Culture** | Stress change - change creates opportunity. | Protect assets/businesses - change can threaten current assets/wealth/products. |
| **Operating Mode** | Action first, then fix mistakes. | Extensive analysis prior to taking action. |
| **Strengths** | New ideas/products. Decision maker(s) close to customers. | Production and marketing ability. |
| **Weaknesses** | Limited experience and resources for mass production and marketing. | Decision makers often removed from customers. |

Incubator

Managing ventures through a relatively small, well planned, internal unit (incubator) within a large organization is an approach which may provide a vehicle for bringing about these marriages. While not a new concept, the approach discussed below redefines an incubator from the more traditional staff organization used to screen prospects, commit funds and monitor developments to an operating unit, with visible ties into the existing organization. The objective of an incubator is to serve as an entry point for new ventures outside the organization's existing core businesses, whether acquired or internal start-ups, and provide them with management and resources until they are large/successful enough to be placed within the company's normal structure.

The incubator's role is not to identify and acquire new opportunities and then become a caretaker or spectator for a portfolio of ventures. Members of an incubator need to possess sufficient operating and marketing experience not only to isolate new business opportunities, but also to review venture activities, provide ongoing assistance to venture management and manage small grass roots units.

In addition to being responsible for new ventures, which normally require cash injections without immediate earnings, an incubator should also manage one or more established business units which, if well managed, will have current earnings. If possible, the management of established business(es) should require similar operating and marketing skills as the start-ups/ventures. Therefore, the established units should be relatively small vs. the corporation's other units, in dynamic markets, with similar processing, etc. If such businesses do not exist within a company, a close proxy should be assigned to the incubator.

Placing an ongoing business in the incubator is important for three reasons:

• Capable operators and marketers need short-term feedback from their activities.

• Often organizations require some short-term measures of progress (earnings) from a group to sustain long-term commitments, particularly during periods of sub-par financial results for the firm.

• Provide a training vehicle for less experienced personnel in the incubator.

81

Mature and/or troubled businesses with a limited future should be excluded. Mature businesses obviously require different skills compared to start-ups and seriously troubled units can take too much of management's time and attention away from its primary role. Also, such a mixed assignment can increase the risk that the corporation's senior management, or even the incubator's management, may begin to focus on short-term results for the entire unit.

---

**As with all organizational undertakings, if an incubator is to be effective, it must have a clear commitment by senior management. An incubator is not a vehicle to "test the water" or to generally "fish around" appearing to look for new growth activities without a serious commitment by the corporation.**

---

Commitment begins with placing proven professionals in the unit from various disciplines such as operations, marketing, finance, etc. To provide assistance to new ventures, either purchased or internal, incubator members must have proven skills, be aware of the support systems within the corporation, have available resources and be given significant autonomy. Since rapid decisions are often required, the necessary level of autonomy may be greater than others at the same level in the organization. Also, members of newly acquired, fully or partially, ventures are likely to be accustomed to dealing with decision makers from other organizations and will expect the same from their new owner or partner. Reporting too low in the organization can be viewed as a major change and a sign of the corporation's lack of commitment.

A successful incubator manager must be trusted by the corporation's management, while probably being viewed as a bit of an outlaw. Since change and growth occur with few fixed rules, the manager must be able to identify the less important corporate norms, which can be violated, but meet the main requirements. A number of large corporations are realizing the value of such managers when placed in especially difficult/extreme or unique situations, such as managing new, fast-paced growth businesses, or playing out an end game strategy.[4]

To demonstrate the importance of the incubator's activity and assure sufficient resources and rapid communications between the company and its ventures, the unit's manager should either be, or report directly to, a senior manager of the parent company. A senior reporting level will also help address the normal problems associated with being viewed by the majority of the parent company's other members as a "special or privileged" group. To the degree that the purpose of the incubator is understood by the average person, its management is known and respected throughout the organization and it is perceived to have support at the highest levels, violations of minor corporate norms will be more generally accepted by the others. This is important not only for the incubator to perform its function but for the general morale of the parent company.

In addition to providing a vehicle for corporate venturing, an incubator can be extremely fertile ground to develop new managers and ultimately to rekindle or strengthen dedication and innovation throughout a company. By including a small select number of less experienced personnel in the group, the incubator can serve as a source of new talent and experience to fill other corporate needs, as well as an avenue to bring people into the organization. Therefore, not only is the organization using the incubator to invest in future businesses, but also to make that ultimate investment, that of selecting and training people. As people move through the incubator into other areas of the corporation and as small businesses grow large enough to be placed into the corporate structure, the company gains from the training of these individuals, as well as their entrepreneurial spirit.

## Keep Your Eyes Open - Benefits & Risks

There should be no rules as to how long a new venture remains part of the incubator. That depends on events such as: the time it takes to develop it into a significant ongoing business, resources required, ability to be integrated into other business units, etc. The establishment of an incubator requires a long-term commitment and patient capital. It must be seen as a vehicle to foster growth for the corporation's future and as an insurance policy against it dying of old age.

The potential benefits of the incubator and the culture it will help to sustain can spread throughout the organization. The most notable of these are:
- Identifying, acquiring and nurturing new growth businesses.
- Training personnel to provide future managers for the corporation.

- Acting as a stimulus and a magnet for new ideas both from internal and external sources.
- Providing the corporation with a "window on technology", thereby multiplying the impact of a firm's R&D expenditures through venturing activities.

The latter point can be more important than it first appears since it may enable an organization to view new technological developments while only investing a portion of the R&D funds. This can be particularly valuable when pursuing higher risk ventures and/or during periods of disappointing financial results for the firm, when R&D funds can suddenly become limited.

It would be foolish to think that an incubator unit is not without risks. The most notable is the need for controls to identify and limit errors while encouraging an entrepreneurial spirit. Due to the number of unknowns and the often rapid changes in technology and/or the marketplace associated with developing a new business, standard measures of performance such as discounted cash flow or payback period used to analyze ongoing, mature businesses can be of limited value. The solution to this rests in three areas:

- Establishing a culture, including a reward system, that encourages an honest, ongoing appraisal of the environment and each venture's future.
- Staffing the incubator unit with trusted, experienced personnel who are less likely to feel their careers are threatened by identifying a problem.
- Providing a periodic formal review, with corporate senior management, to look at overall progress, competitor response, technological changes and other assumptions initially used to justify the new business.

The key to the last step is to provide a system which does not overly focus on current earnings but on the attainment of longer-term goals and trends in the business environment. It must be remembered that growth in its early stages requires cash, non-cash resources and patience. But patience should ultimately be rewarded. Therefore, periodic formal reviews of the underlying assumptions initially used to justify the new venture, as well as those currently being used to continue the business, are essential. This type of system should help segregate delays and temporary disappointments from serious problems. It also provides a forum for venture and corporate management to address structural problems, decide if the business philosophy needs to be modified, or even if it is an opportune time to exit.[5]

# References

1. Tichy, Noel and Charan, Ram, "Speed, Simplicity, Self-Confidence: An Interview with Jack Welch, "Harvard Business Review, September-October 1989. One of numerous discussions/articles on the topic. Older, but, as in many cases, worth reading.

2. Ohno, Taiichi, "Toyota Production System Beyond Large-Scale Production", (Portland, Oregon: Productivity Inc., 1988). It is worth noting that this book was first published in Japan in 1978 and it took ten years to be translated into English. A considerable amount of literature is now available including:

   Liker, Jeffrey K., "The Toyota Way : 14 Management Principles from the World's Greatest Manufacturer," (New York: Mc-Graw-Hill, 2004).

   Spear, Steven and Bowen, Kent H., "Decoding the DNA of the Toyota Production System," Harvard Business Review, September-October 1999.

   Womack, James P. and Jones, Daniel T., "Beyond Toyota: How to Root Out Waste and Pursue Perfection," Harvard Business Review, September-October 1996.

   Peters, Tom, "Thriving on Chaos," (New York: Alfred A. Knopf, Inc., 1987).

3. Walton, Sam and Huey, John, "Sam Walton: Made in America: My Story," (New York: Bantam Doubleday Dell Publishing Group, 1993).

4. Harrigan, Kathryn Rudie, "Managing Maturing Businesses," (Massachusetts: Lexington Books, 1988).

5. For those interested in the process of change and innovation, I recommend: Quinn, James Brian, "Managing Innovation: Controlled Chaos," Harvard Business Review, May-June 1985.

# CHAPTER 6
## PARTICIPATIVE MANAGEMENT - NO FREE LUNCH

Summary

Perhaps no topic in recent times has received as much attention as that of participative management. However, it appears, on average, to remain an area of interest, conversation and experimentation, rather than a concept which is understood and widely practiced. The large scale cutbacks and shutdowns experienced by many organizations have made the implementation of participative techniques more difficult, as members worry daily about their jobs and futures. This heightens suspicions, increasing the normal reluctance to change and reduces peoples' loyalty to their organizations.

Global markets with overcapacity for many products, rising employee costs for businesses (such as health insurance and underfunded pensions) and what has been a general inability to raise prices put continued stress on managers to reduce costs, thus employment in high cost countries. Furthermore, recent experience has demonstrated that, even with increased demand, employment can fall, as the existing excess capacity and productivity gains cover the demand. As an example, years ago I managed a business that, over 3 years, increased production from existing equipment by 20% and member productivity (units produced /hours worked) by 40%, and was profitable before these gains. Despite the gains, due to expanded global competition, a steady increase in the value of the dollar and rising employee costs further efficiencies were required.

People are reminded in the media, despite recent job growth, that this situation may continue, or reappear as, the so-called "Jobless Recovery". Members of Generation X who entered the job market during the Tech Bubble, including expenditures for Y2K, and a period of overstated earnings, felt deceived by the sudden downturn. Job losses have extended beyond manufacturing to include areas such as computer related positions, previously believed to be safe, but now candidates for outsourcing.

The current situation has made the management equation more complex. Senior managers are typically rewarded based on earnings. In the past, jobs were created and general compensation increased, although at some lag, during economic upturns. Thus enabling everyone to benefit. Today, senior managers continue to be rewarded based on financial results, but apparently new jobs and/or overall compensation increases will lag behind historical norms due to productivity gains and perhaps job relocation. This is at a time productivity increases are required which necessitates a focused effort by the entire organization.

As the number of people who have been terminated increased, along with the horror stories of long periods of job hunting, it is disappointing, but reasonable, to expect that some corporate survivors have begun to behave differently. Increases in internal politicking and destructive internal conflict can result. While some members will strive to improve the lot of their organization and its members during difficult times, others will spend an increasing amount, perhaps a majority, of their time "protecting themselves", even at the expense of their peers or subordinates. This disease is extremely difficult to guard against since it can infect all levels, making it all the more important that senior managers be on the lookout for any evidence of such behavior. Only by staying alert and making it absolutely clear to all that this behavior, if it were to occur, would not be tolerated can the organization begin to combat this enemy. If detected, management must take action against this cancer or condemn the organization to a path of increasing internal politicking, conflict and eroding performance.

The benefit from involving as many individuals as possible in the attainment of a goal seems clear, but the commitment and time required to provide an environment where this can be achieved all too often discourages or stops management from developing it. Management must take a number of steps which demonstrate a clear commitment to the process prior to gaining its potential benefits.

Achieving an environment in which members of management and non-management become partners, at least on a limited basis, in operating a business requires the following:

- Shared vision, goals and information;
- Understanding of the importance of the goals and the means by which they are to be achieved;
- Freedom to express views and alternatives and experiment;
- Training;
- Fairness, where all share, not necessarily equally, from successes and failures;
- Planning for people displaced due to occurrences truly beyond their and the organization's control.

If any of the above are missing, management cannot expect the benefits of expanded participation. In fact, by adding several of the vestiges of participative management without providing the basics, people can be expected to respond negatively, as they are likely to perceive such action by management as insincere or self-serving.

We all either know of, or have heard stories about organizations which have achieved seemingly impossible results by increasing the members' participation in such functions as setting or questioning goals and problem identification and solving. Yet, rarely do we consider the amount of effort and commitment required to establish this type of environment. Merely telling people that their participation is welcome is no more effective than periodically stating the importance of quality or safety without installing programs to provide the tools and environment to achieve target levels.

---

**Participative management is no free lunch, but if an organization is to successfully compete, it must find a way of tapping its most vital resource - that of the imagination and creativity of its members.**

---

Shared Vision, Goals and Information

As discussed in Chapter 2, organizations recognized as being better managed understand two basic facts. First, it is impossible for a team to be effective unless it understands and has internalized the goals toward which it is working. Second, information is an asset to be added to and shared by those throughout the organization.

Traditionally, management has seen itself as the source of vision and goal setting, which is shared sparingly with others. The goals established by management were not usually open to discussion, and it was thought that others, "employees", should be satisfied with performing specific tasks assigned by management and had no need to understand the direction of the organization. In addition, information regarding production, costs and overall financial results were usually seen as the privy of management. It appears that management often felt that sharing visions, goals and information somehow reduced or threatened their position.

If for a moment we think about other organizations we belong to, such as clubs, community groups, charities, etc., it becomes clear that people cannot follow goals of which they are not aware. Nor can they make improvements in, say, product quality or costs without sharing sufficient data for them to understand the situation.

---

**As members of these other organizations, we take for granted our ability to discuss goals and have access to information. Yet, when we enter the business arena, management can often act as if this openness is threatening. In reality, such action is not threatening but liberating.**

---

It allows management to explain problems the organization faces and tap the brain power and imagination of others who are the experts at each of their jobs.

Obviously, all information cannot be shared equally throughout the organization and this approach is not meant to create a forum in which management is constantly questioned over every issue. However, with a general environment of openness, this is not likely to occur. Management cannot use this "fear" or "excuse" to forego the opportunity of mobilizing its organization by failing to share its vision and allow it to be modified, as appropriate, based on new information and ideas.

Goals - Understanding Their Importance

Referring to the earlier discussion regarding the importance of work, there appears to be a sound basis for the belief that individuals want to perform actions they see as important. We have findings from people such as Frederick Herzberg, Abraham Maslow, Elton Mayo and Douglas McGregor which can provide an interested manager with an improved understanding of behavior. These works are supported by numerous surveys which continue to point out people's desire to successfully perform tasks that they see as important. If this were not true, why would individuals work so diligently toward the goals of community organizations and charities? Clearly, it is not for monetary compensation, but it provides a means for individuals to pursue goals which they see as meaningful while receiving recognition.

The question needs to be asked, "What does this mean for a manager?" It means that to the best of her ability, part of a manager's job is not only to explain the goals of an organization but also the importance of each individual's and/or group's role in attaining those goals. It also means that recognition must be given to those individuals and/or groups which strive not only to achieve stated objectives, but perform well beyond expectations.

This is not to say that management should try to convince people that unimportant tasks are actually important. Such action results in losing the confidence of members of the organization, since in time they will see through this approach, as well as wasting time and other resources as this tends to continue unimportant tasks. A good self-audit for a manager, in the privacy of his own office or home, is to explain out loud to himself why each function is important. If he is unable to do this to his own satisfaction, he should not attempt it on other members of the organization, but rather question whether the action is needed at all. This audit can aid in stopping two problems. First, as pointed out above, creating meaningless, excess work or trying to "con" fellow workers. Secondly, you may find a task you thought of as unimportant actually is important and this can help stop the elimination of such misunderstood activities.

Freedom to Express and Experiment

People must believe that they can make valid suggestions, receive recognition for good ideas and not suffer reprisal for legitimate errors. While this seems simple, the classical relationship between "management and employee" is that a manager tells the employee what to do and how to do it and the employee performs the tasks. While most of us would agree that this is a very limited view of the relationship, you must consider that this is the history from which modifications to the management-non-management relationship are starting.

Earlier we discussed the importance of ideas and how management can be a self-fulfilling prophecy. Every manager must remind herself of this daily. In the long-run, it is the manager who sets the tone of the relationship. The ability to freely contribute ideas meant to improve an organization must become taken for granted by members. This requires a commitment of time and attitude by management. As a manager, you will do more to enforce participation or to end it by the way you respond the first time an individual makes an unworkable suggestion, an error, or tells you "bad news". For expanded participation to be achieved, people must feel free to bring bad news to supervisors, as early as possible, and to openly discuss solutions.

## Hidden problems are long-term liabilities.

We all admire individuals and organizations that take prudent risks and stick to a long-term program, despite setbacks, and ultimately succeed. Reasonable experimentation must be encouraged among members of the organization. It is only when this freedom is seen as a right by members, with a responsibility by them to use it to improve the organization, that significant gains can be made. This again requires a long-term commitment by management, an understanding that nothing improves if nothing is changed, and a tolerance for failure. Look at the organizations and managements you admire. They probably exhibit these characteristics. Enough said!

Training

One of the requirements for increasing participation, which is frequently overlooked, is a need for training. To a great extent, gone are the days, fortunately, when a "new recruit" watched an "old hand" run a machine for a day before taking his place. We have come to understand that, without documenting a machine's functions, what could go wrong and how to handle the problems, production gains are at best a hit-and-miss proposition.

Adequate training must be provided before a person undertakes any function. While people need the right to experiment and fail, they must be given the tools to succeed. Training is perhaps the most important tool management can initially provide, and it should not be limited only to a routine production process. As we ask people to increase their participation in solving problems, the amount and type of training will increase and change. In addition to providing training for a production process, a new skill such as computer programming, or perhaps meeting remedial needs in reading, training in areas such as interpersonal skills, previously reserved for management, needs to be considered. While organizations are ultimately made up of individuals, improvements generally come about through interaction among individuals or working within a group. Effective training in areas as basic as listening and communicating may, in the long-run, provide surprising results.

**Although the ability to succeed or fail should be seen as each person's right, accompanied by the obligation to improve their organization, management must provide the tools to increase the probability of success.**

People will stop experimenting, and therefore seeking new solutions, if they and others do not enjoy a reasonable amount of success. Continued failure will ultimately discourage seeking improvements. Training is an essential first step in this process. Learning is a vital function for everyone in the organization.

<u>Fairness - Sharing Success and Failure</u>

While the concept of fairness differs among people, we all interpret situations in a context of whether we think people have been treated "fairly". Certainly, if all members of the organization are to play a more active role, it would be reasonable to assume that each of them would derive a portion of the benefits achieved by the whole, as well as those from their individual efforts. It is inconsistent to believe that members of an organization will fully participate if they perceive that groups in the organization will be singled out as privileged. That is not to say that each individual will receive the same compensation or even be compensated in the same manner.

**Members must perceive a general attitude of fairness in the overall approach of rewarding individuals and groups.**

In the same manner that lower, mid-management and non-management personnel are held responsible for performing tasks and contributing improvements, senior management must be held accountable for the strategies that they develop/coordinate and implement. The concept of fairness and compensation received by senior managers in American industry has recently gained a great deal of attention. It is a recurring theme of questions asked to senior executives, as well as a topic for articles usually addressing "needed reforms." In fact, it has become so controversial that some members of government believe legislation may be the only way to guard against potential abuse.

This is not to say that members of an organization, including senior management, should not be rewarded for their contributions. Given the impact of decisions made by senior managers and their actions, it is reasonable to believe that these will have a greater influence on the success of the organization than the average member's actions. But, who could blame the average member of an organization who sees her friend being laid off, therefore increasing her work load, is subject to a wage freeze and lives in day-to-day fear of losing her job from feeling unfairly punished when senior managers measure their compensation in multi-millions of dollars. Even more serious can be a potential situation in which senior managers do not take good, sound business risks to grow their company and improve its future, in order to protect their current high levels of compensation. Such action not only causes the problems you would expect among members, but is also cheating the shareholders of the future of that organization.

As noted earlier, compensation is a very strategic decision. The implications of the compensation system must be fully understood prior to its implementation and need to be routinely reviewed. While the compensation system in many organizations tries to address these issues, there are always examples of companies that are not as diligent. Management cannot expect participation if it rewards itself with multi-millions of dollars based on earnings, stock prices and/or acquisitions and then reduces compensation to others "to become more competitive in the global market." The average person has become increasingly aware of potential abuses and focuses greater attention on it within his own organization.

Bottom Line - Participation is Essential

The bottom line to participative management is that organizations will not prosper unless they can channel the creative efforts of their members. Putting aside an endless discussion about government policies and viewing only the strategic management issues, a brief review of the recent history of America's competitive advantage vs. other nations provides strong evidence of this relationship.

Coming out of WW II, America possessed several major competitive advantages vs. potential foreign competitors. These included:

- A well established, efficient industrial base vs. a decimated industrial structure in most other nations;
- The largest single market of consumers in the world with tremendous pent-up demand built up over the war years;
- An educated, trained work force;
- A universally accepted belief in the high quality of American products;
- Strong consumer confidence in America, its technologies and general ability.

When the above list is compared to the environment in the war-torn nations, it is easy to understand how Americans did not perceive the increased competition that would eventually come from a global marketplace. These advantages not only made it relatively easy for Americans to be successful selling to foreign nations, but reduced the necessity to do business outside its own boundaries due to high internal demand. Given the environment, both management and non-management members were frequently seduced into spending less time worrying about the future, meeting consumer needs and improving product quality. Too often, short-term considerations appear to have been the determining factor in making a decision.

America's relaxed attitude provided other nations with their first strategic advantage. Other advantages included:

- A population committed to rebuilding their nation;
- Base-line technology from American industry which could be modified and improved when building new facilities, therefore ultimately making these facilities more efficient than their American counterparts;
- A long-term competitor, America, that wanted and needed to see this rebuilding and was willing to provide technology and funds.

**The role of committed people in achieving a goal cannot be overstated. Military history proves that a committed, yet understaffed and poorer equipped army can defeat a major power. Why then, are we so surprised when a committed, educated and newly equipped group becomes a world class competitor?**

## No Magic Pill

This book attempts to provide a framework to help a manager draw from known concepts and theories and begin to focus on ways to apply them. It is not a cookbook full of recipes to address every situation you are likely to face. It would be impossible to do this. The environment is too dynamic to be that simple. You must dedicate yourself to understanding your situation and continually focus on improving your organization's abilities. There is no substitute for commitment!

Trust is a must for any meaningful level of participation. Like most things concerning human relations, trust can't be measured, but it is obvious both when it exists and when absent. Recent corporate scandals have hurt the general level of trust of American employees and investors. Remember, employees are your largest investors. In addition to often having financial investments in their employer, they are investing their careers and livelihoods. Management needs to establish or re-establish the general level of trust which previously existed, whether or not they and/or their organization did anything to reduce it. Trust must exist for parties to share thoughts and ideas. Remember the importance people place on work and the role it fills.

An organization must have a vision and concrete plans to achieve it. The vision needs to be openly communicated. The plans need to be monitored, modified as needed and communicated to the degree possible/prudent so as not to jeopardize their success. Compensation is a strategic vehicle in aligning the goals of an organization and its members.

Review your organization's structure to assure that it can execute your plans. Speed is key. Remove any kinks in the communication, production and distribution chains. Participation by those doing the work routinely is essential. Systems such as Toyota's Production System and/or various Lean Systems can be of great assistance in this process. Such a long-term investment cannot be undertaken without an understanding of the process, a clear implementation plan, commitment by management and a sharing with members of its necessity, goals and potential outcome. Introduction of new approaches cannot fail and continually be restarted (some limited modifications are not unusual during implementation) without a loss of trust and commitment. Take time to plan, communicate and commit up front.

Lean Systems rely upon standardization. By standardizing and controlling everything from parts to work practices, a baseline is provided to assure consistency, measure variations in performance and to implement further improvements. Control is used as a means to focus activities on future improvement and process innovation. Rather than being seen as a negative, controls and standardization play a positive role in the improvement process.

Control is a delicate issue. As noted earlier, controls need to identify and limit errors while allowing for an entrepreneurial spirit and providing a basis for improvement. One of my early mentors told me that my greatest challenge as I advanced would be to allow people to make mistakes. The key is to provide controls that play a positive role in improvements by identifying root causes of problems as well as catching situations (mistakes and intentional actions) before they are significant to the organization. For example, a practice of planned job rotation not only broadens people's experience and knowledge (primary goal), but it can also be a subtle control for uncovering problems. While control systems should incorporate more than one level, don't make them too bureaucratic; you will normally lose more than you gain. Mistakes will be made and unfortunately some intentional actions may occur. So will successes.

Do not attack the level of people first. Get rid of the unnecessary work and hidden costs. These can range from inventory costs, packaging, shipping, excess reports, etc. Take time to map your organization's current activities/practices. You may be surprised at what you discover. Learning how you currently operate is a necessary first step to improvement. It is only after non-value adding activities are removed that staffing levels can be rationally addressed. This process is not meant to delay execution but to quickly reduce unneeded costs while gaining information and support for further actions.

Given the economic realities of many organizations, you are likely, at some time, to need to address employee costs and/or levels. A growing company may, even with significant productivity gains, be able to create new jobs fast enough to avoid cutbacks. As some jobs are eliminated, people can be shifted to other areas. Also, as employees gain experience in implementing Lean Systems, they often can prove to be valuable coaches/consultants for implementation elsewhere in the organization. Unfortunately, there will be instances where workforce reductions are necessary.

I hope it is understood that the topics discussed in this book and processes designed to systematically review an organization's activities are not intended to just downsize organizations. In fact, they are aimed at, among other goals, freeing up hidden capacity and increasing creativity which can be the first steps in growth.

---

**Management cannot be satisfied with a cycle of downsizing. This is like a physician watching a patient's health steadily decline over an extended period without making a serious effort to address the problem.**

---

In the case of staff reductions there are usually a limited number of trade-offs. These include: reduction by attrition, part-time employment, reduced benefits, etc. These options should not be used to maintain a long-term, unnecessarily high level of employment which does not provide a benefit to the organization. It is dangerous to use such steps to try to "keep labor peace" and it will always backfire. Having extra personnel available with no plan for their long-term utilization will over time destroy morale and reduce the standards work groups set for and expect of themselves.

If personnel reductions are required, the way management handles them will have a significant impact on those remaining. This can include increases in politicking and self-protection activities, decreases in participation, the most qualified people leaving the organization, or acceptance of the need for downsizing and increases in efficiency. It is my experience that organizations that treat individuals being displaced with understanding and some generosity (severance, retraining, etc.) benefit. The better prepared management is when addressing reductions, the more rational it will act. A diligent management takes steps before it is in financial danger and while it can afford a reasonable separation process. Management needs to stay vigilant and act early. This will provide it with the most options.

Whether addressing changes in compensation or employment levels, employees and/or selected representatives should be included as possible. Participation will help insure that everyone understands the problems and options, thus increasing the probability of the acceptance of management's actions. This step, however, is not taken to reduce management's responsibility to address the problems, but to assist in finding the most workable answers.

Every organization needs to actively seek ways to capture the creativity of its members and have them internalize the organization's goals. To do this, management must be willing to share some of the position it historically has reserved for itself. Non-management members must be willing to take on the responsibility of this shared relationship. Be prepared to be disappointed but stay the course.

---

**People must fear the organization's failure, not the organization itself. An organization possessing a committed membership can make poorer decisions and still be successful, as the dedication and ingenuity of its membership works toward attaining their shared goals.**

---

## References

To expand on the discussions in the chapter:

Bardwick, Judith M., "Danger in the Comfort Zone," (New York: Amacom, 1991).

Bennett, Amanda, "The Death of the Organization Man," (New York: William Morrow and Company, Inc., 1990).

Gertz, Dwight L. and Baptista, Joao, P.A., "Grow To Be Great: Breaking The Downsizing Cycle," (New York: The Free Press, 1995).

Goldratt, Eliyahu M. and Cox, Jeff, "The Goal," (New York: North River Press, Inc., 1984, revised 1986, second revised edition 1992, third revised edition 2004).

Rande, Peter S., Newman, Robert P. and Cavanaugh, Roland, R., "The Six Sigma Way: How GE, Motorola and Other Top Companies Are Honing Their Performance," (New York: McGraw-Hill, 2000).

# CHAPTER 7
## CONCLUDING THOUGHTS - WORK BOOK

Thoughts For Follow-Up

    Listed below are some of the key points discussed in this book. These may be of value to periodically think about. I have found that a quick reminder is often helpful given the numerous interruptions and the hectic pace of our daily lives. Use this chapter as a work book. Add to the statements it contains based on your experiences and insights. Share them with others in the organizations you belong to. The blank pages are for notes. I hope you will need more paper, but, as with this book, it's a start. For years I used any available surface to record ideas. I once completed a transaction on a table cloth in a New York City restaurant. That was an expensive notepad!

    Remember, make time to think and plan before acting, but be sure not to use these steps as an excuse for inactivity or blindly supporting the status quo. Ideas have no schedule. If you mentally play with problems or situations enough, they can "just happen." Results normally follow work. Review your progress, modify actions as required and deal directly with information you acquire. Don't make excuses for problems but identify their cause.

_Notes_

The future of any organization in today's global environment is dependent upon its ability to continuously develop targeted products and improved production and delivery systems, at an ever increasing rate of speed. Without vision and courage, we are hostages of our current situation and random events. Good luck to us all in this learning process!

READY - THINK AND PLAN

(Chapter 1)

IT IS ESSENTIAL THAT MANAGEMENT BE HONEST WITH ITS MEMBERS AS TO THE GOALS AND CONSEQUENCES OF ANY LONG-TERM PROGRAM.

DECISIONS MADE WITHOUT AN UNDERSTANDING OF THEIR RELATIONSHIP TO EACH OTHER AND THEIR LONGER TERM EFFECTS CAN RESULT IN AN UNINTENDED AND UNRECOGNIZED STRATEGY.

AN ORGANIZATION CANNOT AFFORD TO BECOME PARALYZED EITHER BY AN INSUFFICIENT AMOUNT OR AN UNMANAGED GLUT OF DATA.

FREQUENTLY, PRIOR EXPERIENCE AND FORMAL TRAINING HAVE TAUGHT MANAGERS "TO DO" AND NOT TO THINK OR PLAN FOR THE FUTURE.

MANAGERS TYPICALLY HAVE LITTLE FREE TIME TO FOCUS ON PERFORMING THEIR BASIC MANAGERIAL FUNCTIONS OF PLANNING, ORGANIZING, LEADING AND CONTROLLING. THEIR DAYS ARE USUALLY FILLED WITH MEETING NEAR-TERM DEADLINES AND A SERIES OF UNPLANNED BUT CONTINUOUS INTERRUPTIONS.

THE MORE VOLATILE THE ENVIRONMENT, THE GREATER THE NEED TO RECOGNIZE THE DISTINCT ROLE OF MANAGEMENT. ALTHOUGH RARELY OPENLY DISCUSSED, ONE OF THE HARDEST THINGS IN AN ORGANIZATION IS MAINTAINING LONG-TERM GOALS, DISCIPLINE AND ENERGY.

# Notes

CREATION OF AN ENVIRONMENT WHICH ENCOURAGES
PEOPLE TO PERFORM TASKS NOT TO ANY GIVEN
SPECIFICATION BUT TO CONTINUING LEVELS
OF IMPROVEMENT RESULTS IN A PROSPEROUS
ORGANIZATION.

IT SHOULD ALWAYS BE REMEMBERED THAT "BETTER
ORGANIZATIONS" LOOK AT THEMSELVES AS HAVING A
VIRTUALLY INFINITE LIFE AND ESTABLISH SYSTEMS WHICH
WILL PERPETUATE THE LIFE OF THE ORGANIZATION
BEYOND THAT OF ANY INDIVIDUAL OR GROUP.

IT IS A MISTAKE FOR MANAGERS TO BELIEVE THAT EQUAL
TREATMENT IS FAIR. IN FACT, BY TREATING EVERYONE
EQUALLY, YOU PUNISH THE BETTER PERFORMERS AND
REWARD POOR ONES.

BETTER MANAGED ORGANIZATIONS ARE NOT SEDUCED BY
IMPROVED TECHNOLOGY BUT VIEW IT AS A MEANS, WHEN
APPLIED AS PART OF A WELL PLANNED ENVIRONMENT,
TO INCREASE PRODUCTIVITY. ULTIMATELY, PEOPLE'S
IMAGINATION AND DEDICATION TO SOLVING PROBLEMS
ARE THE REAL SOURCE OF ALL PRODUCTIVITY GAINS.

REGARDLESS OF WHAT IS SAID BY MANAGEMENT,
PEOPLE WILL RESPOND TO SIGNALS PROVIDED BY THEIR
ORGANIZATION'S COMPENSATION SYSTEM.

COMPENSATION SYSTEMS ARE LIKELY TO GET THE
RESULTS THEY ARE AIMED AT. SO BE CAREFUL TO SELECT
TARGETS WELL.

BETTER MANAGED ORGANIZATIONS ARE THOSE THAT
RAPIDLY PURSUE WHAT THEY VIEW AS IMPORTANT. WHILE
IT COULD BE ARGUED THAT GENERAL GEORGE PATTON
WAS PREDICTABLE, THE SPEED WITH WHICH HE STRUCK
MADE HIM VIRTUALLY UNSTOPPABLE.

COMMITMENT SHOULD NOT BE MEASURED BY THE
SIZE OF AN ORGANIZATION, BUT BY ITS FOCUS AND
EFFECTIVENESS.

# Notes

COMPETITOR INFORMATION MUST BE SEEN AS AN ASSET
TO BE CONTRIBUTED TO AND SHARED WITH OTHER
MEMBERS OF THE ORGANIZATION.

NO ORGANIZATION IS AT A STEADY STATE; IT IS EITHER
IMPROVING OR DETERIORATING, WHETHER OR NOT
THIS IS OBVIOUS AT THAT MOMENT. IT IS IMPOSSIBLE TO
BE AT A STEADY STATE GIVEN CONSTANT CHANGES IN
MARKETS, COST (INCLUDING LAWS AND REGULATIONS)
AND COMPETITORS.


READY - LEAD AND COMMUNICATE

(Chapters 1-2)

FLATTER ORGANIZATIONS PLACE THEIR MEMBERS ON
NOTICE THAT EACH IS MORE VISIBLE AND THEREFORE
MUST MAKE DECISIONS FOR WHICH THEY WILL BE
ACCOUNTABLE.

ONCE A DECISION IS MADE, THE ACTIVITIES INITIATED
FROM THIS DECISION CAN TAKE ON A LIFE OF THEIR
OWN AND BE FOLLOWED ALMOST BLINDLY TO THEIR
CONCLUSION, EVEN IF SUBSEQUENT EVENTS HAVE
MODIFIED THE DESIRABILITY OF THAT CONCLUSION.

A WELL MANAGED ORGANIZATION KNOWS AND
OUTWARDLY SHOWS THE IMPORTANCE OF ITS MEMBERS
AND INFORMATION, DOES NOT LOSE SIGHT OF THE BASICS
IN ITS BUSINESS AND INDUSTRY, MAKES DECISIONS BASED
ON ITS LONG-TERM VIEW OF THE FUTURE AND MAINTAINS
A SYSTEM WHEREBY DECISIONS ARE MODIFIED AS
EVENTS CHANGE.

THE JOB SOMEONE HOLDS NOT ONLY HAS A DIRECT
BEARING ON THEM WHILE WORKING, BUT ALSO IMPACTS
THEIR PRIVATE LIVES.

_Notes_

GOOD MANAGERS ARE TRAINED, NOT BORN. AN INCREASED AWARENESS TO THE FACTORS AFFECTING PEOPLE'S BEHAVIOR CAN ONLY RESULT FROM A COMMITMENT BY MANAGEMENT.

AT TIMES IT IS EASIER TO LABEL AN ACTION "IRRATIONAL" THAN TO TRY TO UNDERSTAND IT.

WHILE IN CONCEPT MANAGERS REALIZE THAT A REWARD OR PUNISHMENT IS ONLY EFFECTIVE IF THE PERSON RECEIVING IT FEELS REWARDED OR PUNISHED, THE IMPORTANCE OF THIS MATCHING PROCESS IS OFTEN NOT FULLY APPRECIATED.

HERZBERG'S FINDINGS INDICATE THAT THE ONLY EFFECTIVE WAY TO MOTIVATE PEOPLE IS TO GIVE THEM CHALLENGING WORK FOR WHICH THEY ARE QUALIFIED, ALLOW THEM TO ASSUME RESPONSIBILITY FOR THE WORK, AND INDICATE SOME POTENTIAL FOR GROWTH AND ADVANCEMENT.

A DISCIPLINARY OR REWARDING ACTION NEEDS TO BE VIEWED BY EVERYONE AS AUTOMATIC BASED ON THEIR ACTIVITIES.

THE MAJOR ERROR THAT A THEORY X MANAGER FREQUENTLY MAKES IS TO FORGET THAT AN OPEN DOOR POLICY CANNOT WORK WITH A CLOSED MIND.

REMEMBER, AN IDEA IS A VERY PERSONAL POSSESSION. THEREFORE, ACCEPTANCE OF AN IDEA BY MANAGEMENT IS OFTEN VIEWED AS A PERSONAL TRIUMPH AND REJECTION AS A DEFEAT.

A MANAGER WHO FAILS TO UNDERSTAND THE IMPORTANCE OF GROUP MEMBERSHIP, OR SPENDS TIME FIGHTING NORMAL GROUP FORMATION, INCREASES THE PROBABILITY THAT GROUP MEMBERS WILL VIEW THE GOALS OF THE ORGANIZATION AND THOSE OF THE GROUP AS BEING INCOMPATIBLE.

## Notes

INHERENTLY GROUPS ARE NEITHER ANTI NOR PRO
MANAGEMENT. THEY ARE POWERFUL SINCE THEY
INFLUENCE BEHAVIOR OF THEIR MEMBERS.

AIM - FOCUS AND ORGANIZE

(Chapters 3-4)

WITHOUT PREPARATION, ACTING, OR WORSE REACTING,
RATIONALLY AND QUICKLY, ESPECIALLY IN A LARGE
ORGANIZATION IS FREQUENTLY IMPOSSIBLE.

PLANNING REQUIRES A COMMITMENT BY AN
ORGANIZATION TO PERFORM THE NECESSARY RESEARCH
AND A WILLINGNESS TO TAKE A CRITICAL (HONEST) VIEW
OF ITSELF.

TO BE MOST EFFECTIVE, GATHERING AND INTERPRETING
COMPETITOR DATA CANNOT BE VIEWED AS SOMETHING
TO BE DONE ON OCCASION AS THE NEED ARISES.

PARAMOUNT IN A SELF-EVALUATION IS AN
UNDERSTANDING THAT SENIOR MANAGEMENT MUST BE
WILLING TO ACCEPT THE INFORMATION WHICH COMES
FROM A SELF-AUDIT AND EITHER ACT WITHIN THE
IDENTIFIED LIMITS OF THE ORGANIZATION OR CORRECT
THOSE LIMITS.

REMEMBER, AN ANALYSIS OF A MARKET IS NOTHING
MORE THAN A SNAPSHOT IN TIME. CHANGE WILL OCCUR,
WHETHER YOU INITIATE IT OR NOT.

ORGANIZATIONS DO NOT COMPETE AGAINST AN ENTIRE
COORDINATED GROUP OF COMPANIES. FURTHERMORE,
THE QUALITY OF YOUR COMPETITORS IS MORE
IMPORTANT THAN THEIR NUMBER.

# *Notes*

MANAGEMENT NEEDS TO RETURN TO THE QUESTION, "WHAT IS A CUSTOMER BUYING WHEN HE PURCHASES MY SERVICE OR PRODUCT?" IN ORDER TO BROADEN THEIR UNDERSTANDING OF THE MARKET SEGMENTS THEY SERVE AND TO IDENTIFY CURRENT AND FUTURE COMPETITORS.

PEOPLE DO THINGS FOR WHICH THEY ARE REWARDED AND TEND TO AVOID THOSE ACTIVITIES FOR WHICH THEY ARE PUNISHED. THEREFORE, AN ORGANIZATION'S COMPENSATION PROGRAM PLAYS AN INTEGRAL PART IN THE DECISION MAKING PROCESS.

HONESTY ABOUT YOUR ORGANIZATION'S ABILITIES AND LIMITATIONS AND THOSE OF YOUR COMPETITORS IS CRITICAL IN SETTING AN ORGANIZATION'S MISSION AND DEVELOPING AND IMPLEMENTING STRATEGIES.

IF YOU DON'T KNOW WHERE YOU'RE GOING, ANY ROAD WILL GET YOU THERE.
- Source Unknown

AN ACRONYM ALL PRACTITIONERS NEED TO CONSTANTLY REMIND THEMSELVES OF IS "KISS"; KEEP IT SIMPLE, STUPID.

WITHOUT DEDICATED PEOPLE AND A MARKET WHICH BELIEVES A COMPANY'S MANAGEMENT, AN ORGANIZATION CANNOT SURVIVE.

BY TURNING A GLOBAL MISSION STATEMENT INTO SPECIFIC OBJECTIVES WITH AN ASSOCIATED TIMETABLE, MANAGEMENT IS FORCED TO REVIEW THE PROBABILITY OF ATTAINING THESE OBJECTIVES IN LIGHT OF THE ENVIRONMENT AND THEIR AVAILABLE RESOURCES.

_Notes_

REPORTED FINANCIAL RESULTS SUCH AS EARNINGS
ARE DUE TO PAST ACTIVITIES OF THAT ORGANIZATION.
THEREFORE, CURRENT RESULTS MAY ONLY BE VALID
AS AN HISTORICAL MEASURE OF AN ORGANIZATION'S
HEALTH. BE CAREFUL NOT TO SPEND TIME LOOKING
THROUGH A REAR VIEW MIRROR.

TO BE EFFECTIVE, SHORT-TERM OBJECTIVES MUST BE
MEASURABLE EVENTS WHICH DIRECTLY RELATE TO
ACHIEVING LONG-TERM GOALS.

## FIRE - DEMONSTRATE COMMITMENT AND FOLLOW-THROUGH

(Chapters 4-5)

A WELL CONCEIVED STRATEGY DIRECTS THE RESOURCES
OF AN ORGANIZATION AND PROVIDES A FRAMEWORK FOR
DAY-TO-DAY DECISION MAKING.

THE CARDINAL RULE IS TO ASSURE THAT MANAGEMENT
THROUGHOUT THE ORGANIZATION UNDERSTANDS THE
OVERALL GOALS OF THE COMPANY, THEIR ROLE, AND ITS
IMPORTANCE TO THE ORGANIZATION'S SUCCESS.

PROPERLY APPLIED, THE WORD STRATEGY PROVIDES
AN ORGANIZATION WITH A ROAD MAP AS TO WHERE IT IS
GOING AND A MEANS OF ATTAINING ITS GOALS. HOWEVER,
THE WORD STRATEGY CAN ALSO BE USED AS A DEFENSE
FOR LACK OF ACTION OR INAPPROPRIATE ACTION.

ONE OF THE MOST DIFFICULT CHANGES FOR SOME
SENIOR MANAGERS CAN BE THAT THEY MUST VIEW
THEMSELVES AS TEACHERS AND COACHES AND NOT THE
PRIMARY SOURCE OF THINKING AND KNOWLEDGE.

# Notes

JUST AS YOU WOULD NOT BECOME A PARTICIPANT
IN A GAME WITHOUT UNDERSTANDING THE RULES,
MANAGEMENT CANNOT AFFORD TO SELECT AND
IMPLEMENT A STRATEGY WITHOUT COMMITTING
RESOURCES (CAPITAL, FACILITIES AND MANAGEMENT
TALENT), ACCEPTING THE RISK ASSOCIATED WITH THE
STRATEGY AND PROVIDING SUFFICIENT TIME FOR THE
STRATEGY TO WORK.

IT IS IMPORTANT FOR MANAGEMENT TO REALIZE THAT
STRATEGIC MANAGEMENT IS TRANSFERABLE, NOT ONLY
FROM COMPANIES IN THE SAME INDUSTRY BUT FROM
COMPANIES IN NON-RELATED INDUSTRIES.

DUE TO INCREASED TIME DEMANDS, TODAY'S MANAGER
MUST LEARN FROM EVERYDAY OCCURRENCES AND TAKE
THESE LESSONS AND APPLY THEM.

CONTINGENCY PLANNING, LIKE ANY PLANNING ACTIVITY,
IS NOTHING MORE THAN A DISCIPLINED PROCESS TO HELP
INSURE MANAGEMENT FOCUSES ON THE ESSENTIAL ISSUES.

DECISIONS ARE SUBJECT TO THE LAW OF INERTIA AS
WELL AS THE EFFECTS OF NAYSAYERS. A RECOGNIZED
CONTINGENCY PROCESS IS DESIGNED TO OVERCOME
THESE NEGATIVE FORCES.

STRUCTURE MUST BE DRIVEN BY THE BUSINESS AND ITS
STRATEGIES SINCE THIS IS THE VEHICLE THROUGH WHICH
THE ORGANIZATION IMPLEMENTS ITS STRATEGY TO
OBTAIN ITS GOALS.

STRUCTURE AIMS TO PROVIDE TWO SOMETIMES
CONFLICTING ATTRIBUTES - FOCUS AND FLEXIBILITY.

IT CAN BE EXPECTED THAT THE AMOUNT OF TIME
AND EFFORT SPENT IN ACTIVITIES REFERRED TO AS
POLITICKING ARE INVERSELY RELATED TO THE STRENGTH
AND CLARITY OF ANY ORGANIZATION'S STRUCTURE.

# *Notes*

AN AMBIGUOUS ORGANIZATION STRUCTURE CAN UNINTENTIONALLY PROVIDE AN ENVIRONMENT WHERE RISKS, AND THEREFORE OPPORTUNITIES, ARE AVOIDED AS OPPOSED TO ONE IN WHICH RISKS ARE IDENTIFIED AND MANAGED IN ORDER TO IMPROVE AN ORGANIZATION'S OVERALL RETURNS.

IN A POORLY DEFINED ORGANIZATION, INDIVIDUAL OR GROUP VIEWS ARE LIKELY TO BE DEBATED AT VARIOUS POINTS IN THE ORGANIZATION WITHOUT EVER REACHING THE COMPANY'S SENIOR DECISION MAKERS, OR PROVIDED TO THEM ONLY IN CLOSED MEETINGS WITH THE INTENTION OF GAINING SUPPORT FOR A PERSONAL IDEA.

POLITICS IS NOT ONLY DESTRUCTIVE, BECAUSE OF THE IMPACT IT HAS ON INDIVIDUALS AND THE TIME AND RESOURCES IT CONSUMES, BUT MORE IMPORTANTLY, IT HAMPERS THE DECISION MAKING PROCESS.

VIEWING THE POTENTIAL LIFE OF AN ORGANIZATION AS INFINITE FOCUSES ATTENTION ON THE PROBABILITY THAT, OVER THE LIFE OF THE ORGANIZATION, EVERY POSITION IS LIKELY TO BE HELD, AT SOME POINT, BY A PERSON WHO IS NOT FULLY PREPARED TO HOLD IT.

STRATEGY DRIVES STRUCTURE. WITHOUT A CLEAR VISION AND STRATEGY, SELECTING THE PROPER STRUCTURE IS A HIT OR MISS PROPOSITION.

MANAGEMENT WHICH FOCUSES LARGELY ON TODAY'S ACTIVITIES WITHOUT A DIRECTION OF WHERE THEY ARE LEADING THE ORGANIZATION WILL WIND UP CONTINUALLY MODIFYING ITS STRUCTURE ON AN AD HOC BASIS. THIS CAN LEAD TO CONFUSION ON THE PART OF ITS MEMBERS, INCREASE PEOPLE'S ANXIETY RELATING TO THEIR JOB RESPONSIBILITIES AND CAREERS, AS WELL AS INCREASE THE PROBABILITY THAT THE NECESSARY RESOURCES TO MANAGE THE BUSINESS(ES) ARE NOT DELIVERED IN AN EFFICIENT MANNER.

# Notes

EITHER CONSCIOUSLY OR UNCONSCIOUSLY, STRUCTURE
WILL ULTIMATELY SHOW MANAGEMENT'S PLANS OR
VISIONS FOR THE ORGANIZATION AND ITS BELIEF AS
TO THE IMPORTANCE OF UNITS/FUNCTIONS IN THAT
ORGANIZATION.

THE NECESSARY RESOURCES FOR AN ORGANIZATION
GO BEYOND THOSE NORMALLY THOUGHT OF, SUCH
AS MONEY. THEY INCLUDE, TIME, AS WELL AS THE
COMMITMENT OF COMPETENT PEOPLE AND TRAINING.

TECHNOLOGY CAN BE ACQUIRED OR COPIED BY
COMPETITORS, BUT A CULTURE THAT SIMPLIFIES
COMMUNICATION AND INCREASES SPEED CAN
TAKE YEARS TO ACQUIRE, IF AT ALL. THIS IS A REAL
COMPETITIVE EDGE.

YOU CANNOT BLAME A CUSTOMER FOR GOING TO
ANOTHER ORGANIZATION TO SATISFY HER NEEDS IF YOU
DON'T. THAT IS EXACTLY WHAT YOU WOULD EXPECT AN
EDUCATED CONSUMER TO DO IN A GLOBAL MARKET.

IF YOU RESPOND TO HIS NEEDS, THE CUSTOMER HAS
A CHOICE OF WORKING WITH A PROVEN, RESPONSIVE
PARTNER OR TRYING TO START UP A NEW RELATIONSHIP
WITH YOUR COMPETITOR.

CUSTOMERS KNOW MORE ABOUT THE VALUE OF YOUR
PRODUCT THAN YOU DO.

ULTIMATELY, DIRECT CONTACT IS VITAL TO FOSTER TRUST
AND AN EXCHANGE OF INFORMATION/PERCEPTIONS.

THE EXISTING CULTURE IN LARGE, HIERARCHICAL
STRUCTURES HAS, AS ONE OF ITS OBJECTIVES, THE
CONTINUATION OF MUCH OF THE STATUS QUO WHILE
SMALLER/VENTURE COMPANIES ARE DEDICATED TO
CHANGE.

_Notes_

AS WITH ALL ORGANIZATIONAL UNDERTAKINGS, IF AN INCUBATOR IS TO BE EFFECTIVE, IT MUST HAVE A CLEAR COMMITMENT BY SENIOR MANAGEMENT. AN INCUBATOR IS NOT A VEHICLE TO "TEST THE WATER" OR TO GENERALLY "FISH AROUND" APPEARING TO LOOK FOR NEW GROWTH ACTIVITIES WITHOUT A SERIOUS COMMITMENT BY THE CORPORATION.

## FIRE - KEEP EVERYONE INVOLVED

(Chapter 6)

PARTICIPATIVE MANAGEMENT IS NO FREE LUNCH, BUT, IF AN ORGANIZATION IS TO SUCCESSFULLY COMPETE, IT MUST FIND A WAY OF TAPPING ITS MOST VITAL RESOURCE - THAT OF THE IMAGINATION AND CREATIVITY OF ITS MEMBERS.

AS MEMBERS OF CLUBS, COMMUNITY GROUPS AND CHARITIES, WE TAKE FOR GRANTED OUR ABILITY TO DISCUSS GOALS AND HAVE ACCESS TO INFORMATION. YET, WHEN WE ENTER THE BUSINESS ARENA, MANAGEMENT CAN OFTEN ACT AS IF THIS OPENNESS IS THREATENING. IN REALITY, SUCH ACTION IS NOT THREATENING BUT LIBERATING.

HIDDEN PROBLEMS ARE LONG-TERM LIABILITIES.

ALTHOUGH THE ABILITY TO SUCCEED OR FAIL SHOULD BE SEEN AS EACH PERSON'S RIGHT, ACCOMPANIED BY THE OBLIGATION TO IMPROVE THEIR ORGANIZATION, MANAGEMENT MUST PROVIDE THE TOOLS TO INCREASE THE PROBABILITY OF SUCCESS.

MEMBERS MUST PERCEIVE A GENERAL ATTITUDE OF FAIRNESS IN THE OVERALL APPROACH OF REWARDING INDIVIDUALS AND GROUPS.

# *Notes*

THE ROLE OF COMMITTED PEOPLE IN ACHIEVING A GOAL CANNOT BE OVERSTATED. MILITARY HISTORY PROVES THAT A COMMITTED, YET UNDERSTAFFED AND POORER EQUIPPED ARMY CAN DEFEAT A MAJOR POWER. WHY THEN ARE WE SO SURPRISED WHEN A COMMITTED, EDUCATED AND NEWLY EQUIPPED GROUP BECOMES A WORLD CLASS COMPETITOR?

MANAGEMENT CANNOT BE SATISFIED WITH A CYCLE OF DOWNSIZING. THIS IS LIKE A PHYSICIAN WATCHING A PATIENT'S HEALTH STEADILY DECLINE OVER AN EXTENDED PERIOD WITHOUT MAKING A SERIOUS EFFORT TO ADDRESS THE PROBLEM.

PEOPLE MUST FEAR THE ORGANIZATION'S FAILURE, NOT THE ORGANIZATION ITSELF. AN ORGANIZATION POSSESSING A COMMITTED MEMBERSHIP CAN MAKE POORER DECISIONS AND STILL BE SUCCESSFUL, AS THE DEDICATION AND INGENUITY OF ITS MEMBERSHIP WORKS TOWARDS ATTAINING THEIR SHARED GOALS.